PROLOGUE

This is a story of war. It is also the story of one man's dream. It is a story from the deepest past, and yet it is a story as close to us as the wind.

Across the marsh and scrub that lie along the edge of the Kara Menderes, the modern name for the river that was known in ancient times as the Scamander, stands a nondescript hillside called Hissarlik. In the nineteenth century it was overgrown, the haunt of owls, foxes, vipers, hawks and other predators. But this hill was transformed because of the dream of a German businessman called Heinrich Schliemann. He believed that *The Iliad*, the epic poem written by Homer that takes as its subject the last days of the siege of Troy, was based on real historical events. Academics poured scorn on Schliemann's idea – for centuries scholars had believed that both the place depicted and the events in the epic were mere fables. But nothing would change the mind of this man – he was determined to find the city of Troy.

The narrative of the epic is set in the period around 1250BC, shortly before the Mycenaean civilization of the Mediterranean began to crumble and city states such as Thebes, Knossus and Tiryns fell victim to a period when settled life broke down. It took centuries to rebuild the glory that had been lost. It was a true dark age, but through travelling storytellers and the oral tradition, the stories of old heroes and gods, among them tales of the siege of Troy, were kept alive.

For centuries scholars believed that both the place depicted and the events in the epic were mere fables. It took an unscholarly German indigo salesman to make the connection between the text of *The Iliad*, as written down by Homer, and the truth. He discovered site of an ancient city that could have been the real Troy.

On one side of the channel that was once called the Hellespont, and is now known as the Dardanelles, the Scamander winds across the plain and opens out into the sea. Across the channel and the Aegean Sea, the waters over which Greek warriors sailed to avenge the wrong done to Menelaus of Sparta, lies northern Greece, while at the opposite end, the strait emerges into the Sea of Marmara. Beyond the Scamander there is a ridge of hills that have witnessed a more modern conflict, for these hills lead on to Gallipoli, where one of the most brutal episodes of the First World War took place.

A city certainly existed at Hissarlik at the time in which the epic is set, as it had done for centuries before. Heinrich Schliemann was convinced that the city he uncovered was the city of Troy. The site is a place of magic. It is a place where you can listen to the wind and hear the sound of shield on shield, bronze on bronze, sword on sword and the cries of dying men.

The story seems as old as time and yet it is as fresh as the poppies covering the land like gouts of blood. Hawks hurtle down to shatter the skulls of their prey on the fallen stones that are all that is left of the city – except for the story. Listen to the wind and you may hear a tale in which myth and history mix, a tale that has been told again and again for more than three thousand years. This book tells the story of that epic and of the discovery of the real city called Troy.

CAST OF CHARACTERS

Mythical characters refuse to be pinned down. You may read one mythological dictionary and find a set of references re-telling a Greek myth, only to find that the characters behave in quite a different way in another version. But that, in its way, is the glory of these stories. Nothing is set in stone, which ensures that Greek mythology is rich terrain for a storyteller.

Troy does not re-tell every tale in *The Iliad*, instead relating some of the epic's key episodes. This is a brief guide to some of the characters (both mortal and immortal) mentioned in this book – there are many more that make up the tapestry of Greek mythology.

HEROES, MEN AND WOMEN

ACHILLES

Son of Thetis and Peleus, Achilles is the greatest Greek hero. His wrath, caused when Agamemnon steals his companion, Briseis, is one of the major themes of *The Iliad*.

AENEAS

Aeneas is the son of Aphrodite and Anchises. He comes from Dardania to fight against the Greeks and is related to Priam of Troy. Married to Creusa, he survives the fall of Troy to found the city of Rome.

AGAMEMNON

The King of Mycenae and leader of the Greek army, Agamemnon is the brother of Menelaus. He is married to Clytemnestra.

AJAX

Greek hero, sometimes known as Aias.

ANCHISES

King of Dardania, Anchises is father of Aeneas and kinsman of Priam.

ANDROMACHE

Wife of Hector and mother of Astyanax, Andromache's father and brothers are killed by the Greeks during the siege of Troy. She is emblematic of the suffering of women during war.

BRISEIS

Concubine of Achilles, she is stolen by Agamemnon at the beginning of *The Iliad*, causing Achilles to withdraw from fighting the Trojans.

CALCHAS

The seer who accompanies the Greek army to Troy.

CHRYSEIS

Daughter of Chryses, she is brought to the Greek camp by Agamemnon. Her abduction and the subsequent treatment of her father by the Greek High King bring pestilence on the troops, so she is returned to her home. In return Agamemnon steals Briseis from Achilles, incurring his wrath.

CHRYSES

Priest of Apollo and father of Chryseis, he begs for the return of his daughter when she is abducted by Agamemnon. When the Greek king refuses, he prays to Apollo and brings plague on the Greeks.

DEIPHOBUS

The son of Priam and the brother of Paris and Hector.

DIOMEDES

Greek hero and friend of Odysseus. He was one of the failed suitors of Helen and one of the Greeks who stole into Troy within the Wooden Horse.

HECTOR

Son of Priam, Hector is one of the bravest of the Trojan heroes. His killing of Patroclus brings Achilles back into the field of battle and ends in his slaughter by the Greek hero.

HELEN

"The most beautiful woman in the world", Helen is the daughter of Zeus, who came to her mother, Leda (or in some versions Nemesis), disguised as a swan. Helen is the wife of Menelaus and is abducted by Paris, who takes her to Troy.

IDOMENEUS

A Greek warrior and King of Crete.

MEMNON

An Ethiopian warrior who fights on the side of the Trojans and is killed by Achilles.

MENELAUS

King of Sparta, Menelaus is brother of Agamemnon and husband of Helen. He competes for the hand of Helen with many suitors, who then band together to support him when she is abducted by Paris.

NESTOR

The King of Pylos, Nestor is a wise Greek warrior.

ODYSSEUS

A Greek hero and the King of Ithaca, in some versions of the myths Odysseus is responsible for the idea of the Wooden Horse. Married to Penelope, his ten-year journey home from the Trojan War is the subject of *The Odyssey*. In Latin his name is Ulysses.

PARIS

Son of Priam, Paris is brought up by a shepherd on Mount Ida after a prophecy reveals that he will bring about the destruction of Troy. When he names Aphrodite "the fairest" in a challenge, the goddess promises Paris the hand of Helen. He abducts Helen while on a mission to Sparta, triggering the siege of Troy.

PATROCLUS

Beloved friend of Achilles, Patroclus is slain by Hector. Achilles, who has withdrawn from battle, returns to the conflict as a result of his friend's death.

PELEUS

Greek hero and king of Phthia, Peleus is the father of Achilles and husband of Thetis.

PRIAM

The King of Troy and father of many sons, including Hector, Paris and Deiphobus, Priam is the husband of Hecuba.

GODS AND GODDESSES

Names in brackets refer to the Roman names for some of the Greek deities.

APHRODITE (VENUS)

Aphrodite represents love; in some versions of the myths she is the daughter of Zeus, in others she is born of the ocean. She is a pivotal in the story of Troy, as her promise to Paris that he shall have the hand of Helen brings about the war. She is married to Hephaestus, but takes many lovers including Ares and Anchises, with whom she has a son, Aeneas.

APOLLO

Represented by the Sun, Apollo "the brilliant" is the son of Zeus and Leto. He is the god of prophecy and of music.

ARES (MARS)

The god of war, Ares is the son of Zeus and Hera, and the lover of Aphrodite.

ATHENA (MINERVA)

A virgin goddess, Athena is known as the "grey-eyed". She is a war goddess, but is also the guardian of cities – the Trojans worshipped her. The capital of Greece takes her name.

HEPHAESTUS (VULCAN)

The lame god of fire, Hephaestus is the son of

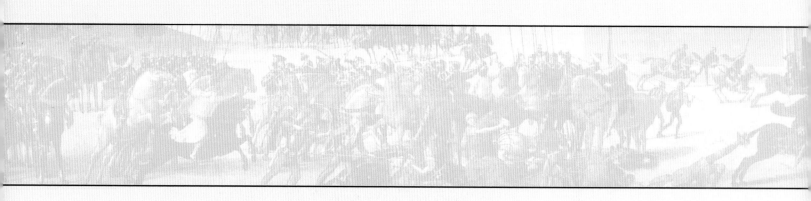

THIS IS A CARLTON BOOK

First published in 2004
This edition published in 2018 by Carlton Books Ltd
A division of the Carlton Publishing Group
20 Mortimer Street
London W1T 3JW

A CIP catalogue for this book is available from the British Library.

ISBN 978 1 78739 091 1

Printed in Dubai

TROY

THE MYTH AND REALITY BEHIND THE EPIC LEGEND

Nick McCarty

CARLTON
BOOKS

CONTENTS

◆◆

MAP OF HOMER'S TROY

Zeus and Hera and the husband of Aphrodite. Brought up by Thetis, Hephaestus is a superb craftsman, making the magical shield with which Achilles goes into battle.

HERA (JUNO)

The wife, and perhaps sister, of Zeus, Hera is one of the most powerful of the gods of Olympus and is the mother of many children including Ares and Hephaestus.

HERMES (MERCURY)

The winged messenger of the gods, Hermes is the son of Zeus. He leads the goddesses, Aphrodite, Hera and Athena, to Paris on Mount Ida.

POSEIDON (NEPTUNE)

God of the sea, and brother of Zeus, Poseidon is a powerful and mighty deity, second only to his brother. He has the power to make earthquakes and lives beneath the ocean.

THETIS

A sea goddess, Thetis is the mother of Achilles and the wife of Peleus.

ZEUS (JUPITER, JOVE)

The greatest of the Greek gods, Zeus, the "thunder maker", is the husband of Hera and father, among others, to Helen, Ares and Athena. Zeus stands for balance and justice and holds ultimate power over all Greek deities and mortals.

CHAPTER ONE

WHO WAS HOMER?

Heinrich Schliemann was certain that the lost city of Troy existed somewhere in Greece or on the coast of Turkey. So if the legendary city of Troy existed, then what about Homer?

The poet Homer is first named in the work of the philosopher Xenophanes (c.570–480BC). The Greek historian Herodotus (c.480–c.425BC) claims that Homer was born about 850BC. He is quoted by the great philosophers Plato (c.428–348BC) and Aristotle (384–322BC) among others. However, despite such references to him, solid information about Homer has never been found. He may have been born in Smyrna, a Greek colony, which spread along what is now part of the Turkish coast. Tradition claims that Homer was blind and told his stories while travelling from town to town.

The subject matter of Homer's best-known epics stems from the Trojan War. *The Iliad* tells of the last days of the siege of Troy, and *The Odyssey* is the tale of the hero Odysseus's ten-year journey home after the war had ended. The stories are filled with action and detail that reflect the lifestyle and the social mores of Homer's time. This was a period when the Greeks had settled down after a dark age and these epics of the oral tradition were finally written down.

HISTORY AND THE ORAL TRADITION

The story told in *The Iliad* is of events that probably happened in about 1250BC. It has been calculated that the epic story as we know it was finalized – or at least written down – in about 725BC, some five centuries later.

This long gap between the actual events and the written document affects the way the story is told and, of course, its historical accuracy. However, it is likely that the root of the story lies in reality. An attack by the Mycenaean Greeks on Troy probably did happen during the period in which much of the material that emerged as *The Iliad* began to be told.

There has long been argument about the number of Homer's sources. Even as written down, the tale is clearly derived from the oral tradition, with many strands, sources and embellishments. The story that forms the core of *The Iliad* was sung and told over the centuries by bards and storytellers, just as the traditional epics of the Celts and the sagas of the Vikings in Iceland were passed from one generation to another. At the same time, fragments from other cultures and myths from surrounding nations may well have augmented the story. The tales resemble a vast, almost cosmic, soap opera, which was elaborated with each new telling. One device of these storytellers was the use of repetitions and unchanging descriptions of people and places. These stylized reiterations were oral tricks, giving the storyteller the chance to

ABOVE *Homer. A marble bust* (AD1–2) *of the poet and author of* The Iliad *and* The Odyssey. *Current opinion suggests that he lived in Greece around 700BC.*

OPPOSITE *A detail from "The Siege of Troy" by Biagio di Antonio (1476–1504). It shows Hector being dragged around the walls of Troy.*

TROY: A TIMELINE

1250BC

Traditional date of the Trojan War.

1200BC

End of Mycenaean civilization in Crete.

1100–800BC

A "dark age" for Greece. The cause of the obliteration of the city states of Mycenae, Sparta, Tiryns and Thebes is uncertain. One theory is that it was as a result of continual wars either between themselves or with more distant cities, such as Troy. Whatever the reason, there was destruction throughout the Greek city states, including the loss of crafts, such as writing, widespread migration of the population and famine.

725–675BC

The Iliad and *The Odyssey* are composed. This was a period that saw a resurgence of cultural life in the Greek city states – an age of individualism and egalitarianism.

Cities were no longer controlled by military oligarchies but were ruled by or with the consent of the people. In this liberal climate poets such as Homer could create and record the tales they heard. Tales of a mythical past were there to be written down, to be embroidered and expanded by poets of the time. Poets wrote about the last great exploits of their Mycenaean forebears, while at the same time reflecting their own times. So the power struggle between Achilles and Agamemnon in *The Iliad* is also a mirror of the attitudes of the poet's era.

think about the path the story would take next or allowing him a moment to gather his thoughts before embarking on the next part of the narrative.

Homer was the poet who pulled together the many strands, additions, incidents, hymns and descriptions of the storytellers into a coherent and truly epic form. He maintained the repetitions from the oral tradition and used them as a poetic device. The names and attributes of the gods' and heroes' characters colour the piece, so we have descriptions such as Thetis of the "silver feet"; Hector, the "horse tamer"; Achilles, the "fleet-footed"; Helen of the "long hair" and Odysseus, the "fox", repeated throughout the tale.

Scholars once claimed that the epic was entirely the work of one poet, although it now seems more probable that it was the work of several people. Even if an individual called Homer did not create the whole story, there was a point at which the tales were moulded into such a powerful shape that *The Iliad* has never diverted from that form since. Whether an individual or a group of poets, "Homer" made the many oral stories read as they were created by a single voice. The genius of this was to create a world in the epic poem that reflected the cultural, religious, familial and religious standards of the period in which the verse was written down, while telling a tale set long before.

HOMER'S TROY

Homer's historic Troy is a rich and teeming city, standing as a trading post between Asia and the Mediterranean. This is an image reinforced by the artefacts discovered on the site of the city that was uncovered by Heinrich Schliemann. The city attracted trade from the hinterland as well as being a location from which goods could be sent by sea to the islands and mainland of Greece across the Aegean Sea. Troy was a powerful city state that probably profited from every merchant who passed along the local trade routes of the time. It was a toll gate on the Hellespont.

Homer gave listeners – and later, readers – details about weapons, food, religious practices, gods, marriage and death garnered from their own times. Battles are described as if they were happening in Homer's world. Much of the true history of the period of the Trojan War is lost as a result of the dark age when records were not kept. However, the oral tradition of the Greeks kept some of the facts alive, mixing them with tales of heroes, heroines and gods.

So Homer tells his story from the perspective of his time looking back across that dark age to a glorious period many centuries before. For example, the place of the gods in the lives of mortals is recorded very much from Homer's perspective, and not as it would have been for Agamemnon or Priam, Hector or Achilles. In effect, the story is told to suit the audience of the time.

Thousands of years later, a short, bad-tempered, plain and greedy German businessman, Heinrich Schliemann, took the work of Homer, believing beyond doubt that the historical site of Troy could be found by a careful analysis and re-reading of the words of *The Iliad* and *The Odyssey*. In fact, in many ways this arrogant individual was using the words to suit his own beliefs and create his own myth of Troy.

CHAPTER TWO

SCHLIEMANN'S QUEST

The son of a poor clergyman, Heinrich Schliemann was born in a small village in Mecklenburg, Germany, on January 6, 1822. As a child, he was sent to work in a grocer's shop without enjoying much of an education; the family needed his small wage. Schliemann's mother died when he was nine and the village learned that his father had been conducting an affair with a maid.

The pastor was, of course, turned out of the community as an unsuitable person to tend to the little flock. Schliemann was sent away and separated from his sister.

Schliemann began a period of wandering, as he struggled to make a living. It was about this time that he was given a book that was to change his life – *The Iliad*. He read and re-read the epic tale, believing even then that it was an historical and factual document as much as it was a myth.

For years he travelled the world, moving from Java to Amsterdam, from Hamburg to St Petersburg. Wherever he travelled, he made it his business to learn the local language – Schliemann was a man desperate to learn, desperate for knowledge. He was also becoming a man who relied on his own wit and determination to make his way in the world. Nothing was going to stand in the way of this short, bumptious German.

Schliemann was concerned that he had to remain healthy in order to make his way in the world. He didn't smoke or drink and whenever he could he swam every day in cold water. He appears to have been a very successful businessman: wherever he ventured money it made more. In 1846 he became a dealer in commodities in Russia, where he married. Three children followed, including a son to whom Schliemann wrote boastful letters almost all his life. However, the marriage was a failure.

Schliemann travelled to America, in order to take advantage of the divorce laws. Between journeys that took in New York, California and Mexico, he managed to set his divorce in motion and to become an American citizen.

In 1866 Schliemann, now rich and successful, enrolled as a part-time student at the prestigious Sorbonne University in Paris. The greying millionaire sat among the young students and took a range of courses, including modern French, poetry, Arabic and Greek philosophy. This single-minded man spoke seven languages fluently and, like so many driven men, he was ruthless in his determination to get what he wanted. The stories of the Greek and Trojan warriors still filled his head as they had when he was a boy. In Schliemann's view, Homer was more an historian than a poet. The palaces and the walls of Troy, the fleet of ships on the beach outside the city walls, the battles, defeats and victories that Homer described were, he believed, all rooted in history. Schliemann would use *The Iliad* like a Baedeker guidebook. Academics might scoff, but this didn't put him off. Others might think him unhinged... he ignored them. He was going to discover the true location of Troy.

OPPOSITE *The ruins of Troy and the view across the plain towards the River Scamander.*

BELOW *Heinrich Schliemann, aged 55, in a portrait painted by Sidney Hodges.*

RIGHT *The mound of Hissarlik, the site of the city of Troy. (3000–1100BC). Note the fortifications and the narrow entrance between the walls.*

At the site of Hissarlik, in northwest Turkey, Schliemann dug and discovered a rich hoard of archaeological treasures. In particular he found what he claimed to be "Priam's Gold". Other more skilled – and certainly more meticulous – archaeologists have dug on the same site and confirmed that the hill is the site of nine cities, built one on top of another. It was in the second layer of the site, labelled Troy 2, that Schliemann believed he had discovered the Troy of *The Iliad*. It was a momentous discovery that destroyed the prejudices of the blind academics who had mocked him.

FORTIFIED CITY

The layers that were uncovered contained evidence of a fortified city that had existed on the site from 3000BC through to AD400, when it lost any importance it had as a centre for trade. By then, the Roman Emperor, Constantine, had built his capital on the site of Byzantium to the east, a great trading city, which later became known as Constantinople.

Over time the mighty walls of the outer city at Hissarlik were neglected and began to crumble. Those of the inner city had long been destroyed by fire and buried. It was the evidence of these burned walls, as much as the artefacts and treasures he found, that led Schliemann to believe one of these layers was the Troy of King Priam, the walls of which had protected the lovely Helen from the anger of her husband, Menelaus.

Over time, these walls and the houses and streets within, had become the homes of many animals and reptiles, including foxes, bats, martens and snakes. The blocks of stone that had formed the city had been removed and used to build other houses or walls and, as time went by, the hill was slowly buried under scrub and earth. It was no longer known as Troy, if it ever had been. Troy no longer existed except in the epic poem about the siege and war. It vanished into myth.

But Heinrich Schliemann had been convinced from childhood that the myth was real, and he was determined to find the home of his heroes. He was convinced that he would bring that mythic city to life again. In many ways, his story is as epic as that of Troy itself.

Without the travelling storytellers who listened, remembered and refashioned the epic, Homer would have known nothing of this story of love and anger, fighting, bravery and terrible revenge. If he hadn't recorded the story for posterity we would know little or nothing about the Trojan War. But without Schliemann we would know nothing of the city that many believe is the site of the real Troy.

Troy is as much a figment of the imagination as it is the structure built of rock and clay that existed in Hissarlik. It is as much the ancient tale that Homer re-tells, as it is an ancient town that swarmed with men and women who cooked on stone hearths; stored oil in vast earthen pots and bought and sold magnificent golden diadems and jewellery fine enough for the most beautiful woman in the world to wear.

When Schliemann first came to Hissarlik in 1869 all that remained of the city that had once stood there was a small, unimposing jumble of rocks and earth. But in his mind he saw the city that Homer had described:

ABOVE *An image incised into a bronze Etruscan mirror dating from the fourth century* BC. *It show Menelaus and Helen of Sparta.*

> *… beyond the plain, to one side the River Scamander curved. On the other side stood the sloping, mighty walls of Troy. On one side the thousand curved boats drawn up on the sand and on the other the vast wooden gates of the city. Inside these walls King Priam reigned and his sons Hector and Paris slept. Beside the boats, men from the island and city states, from Sparta, Crete, Athens, Ithaca or Corinth slept. Odysseus and Achilles, Agamemnon, Ajax and Menelaus – lay wrapped in their boat cloaks and waited for the dawn that would bring another battle and the darkness of death. These were the Achaean {Greek} hordes bent on vengeance.*

And why did the Greeks come to the sloping, mighty walls of Troy? It all began with a betrayal.

CHAPTER THREE

THE ROOTS OF WAR

◆▪◆

It could be said that the Trojan War began when Priam, King of Troy, was told his unborn son would cause the downfall of his great city. Or perhaps it began with a challenge on a hillside where half-wild bulls were herded.

A GOLDEN APPLE

Priam kept a number of wives, chief of whom was Hecuba, mother of many sons including the great hero, Hector. Shortly before she gave birth to Paris, a prophecy foretold that the unborn child would destroy Troy if he were allowed to live. When the child was born, Priam and Hecuba gave him to a shepherd with instructions to leave him to die on the slopes of Mount Ida. It was an act for which Priam felt extreme guilt.

However, the shepherd disobeyed his king and brought Paris up as his own. The boy lived free and wild on the slopes of the mountain, tending the half-wild cattle. As he grew up, Paris became the most handsome of young men, marrying a nymph called Oneone, and living in ignorance of his illustrious parentage.

Soon, Paris was to face a challenge that would change his simple life. A party was given to celebrate the marriage of the sea-goddess Thetis to the mortal Peleus. All the gods and goddesses were invited to the wedding, except for one, the mischief-making Eris. She was determined to wreak her revenge for the insult and sneaked into the wedding party where she threw a golden apple onto the wedding table. On it was written: "for the most beautiful".

There were three great goddesses at the table: Hera, the goddess of marriage and childbirth; Athena, the goddess of war; and Aphrodite, the goddess of love. They argued about who should have the apple and to stop the wedding descending into chaos, Zeus, the chief of the gods, told them that they could settle the matter by asking a young man – Paris – to answer the question.

Accompanied by Hermes, the messenger of the gods, Hera, Athena and Aphrodite went to meet Paris. They grew colder as they climbed high into the green pastures of Mount Ida, wrapping their scarves about their faces. They found Paris looking after the wild, horned cattle. Hermes told the young man that he had to choose the most beautiful of the three goddesses, who were presented to him in mortal form.

Paris was not happy. He knew that whatever he said would be wrong. He tried to refuse but Hermes reminded him that Zeus, the greatest of all gods, had ordered him to choose – he could not disobey the mighty Thunder Maker.

Hermes gave the young man the golden apple and the three goddesses uncovered their faces. Paris was nearly blinded by their loveliness. He panicked, and suggested he split the apple into three to give each goddess an equal share. Hermes refused – Paris must choose; he was trapped.

Each of the goddesses made Paris an offer. Hera stood in front of him first and told him that she would make him a king, richer than any other man if he bestowed the apple upon her. Paris said nothing.

Athena was next. She promised him victory in all his battles, and that he would be the wisest man in the world should Paris to give the apple to her. Paris smiled and said, "I'm a herdsman. What have I to do with battles?"

Over their heads the mountain crags climbed into the deep blue of the sky and eagles soared among the snow-capped peaks. The soft summer wind blew through the sweet smelling grass. Aphrodite stood close to the trembling Paris, smiled and promised Paris the hand of Helen of Sparta, daughter of Zeus and the most beautiful woman in the world. The young man didn't need to think. He gave Aphrodite the golden apple, and in that instant made enemies of Hera and Athena. It is this myth, the Judgement of Paris, that begins the events that Homer was to write down as *The Iliad*.

PARIS RETURNS TO TROY

But despite Aphrodite's promise Paris was still a humble shepherd. How was he to meet the most beautiful woman in the world? By returning to Troy.

LEFT *A sixteenth-century painting showing "The Judgement of Paris". The youth had to choose the most beautiful goddess – it is a terrible dilemma for a mere mortal.*

Every three years Priam hosted a festival on the plains in front of his city. Prizes were given to poets, singers and artists but above all to the athletes who came from far and wide to compete in the games held there. Paris had never been allowed to attend these games, as his guardian was afraid the boy would be recognized. The shepherd had always known that he was in grave danger if this ever happened. To disobey the king was a crime and for a mere shepherd to do so would almost certainly lead to his execution. The shepherd was not only kind-hearted, he was also a brave man. He had the very best reasons for making sure that the king never saw the handsome young man. Paris, of course, had no idea of the danger he was putting his guardian in. He was determined to go to the games without telling the old man, leaving the mountain in secret one morning.

Paris entered three races, winning the first with ease. One of Priam's other sons, Deiphobus, came second. He was not pleased. The brothers ran against each other in the second race and Paris won again. The crowd in the stadium buzzed – who was this unknown young man who could so easily defeat the mighty Deiphobus? The king's son challenged the mysterious youth to a final race.

They began together but Paris soon raced ahead and won again. The furious Deiphobus turned and reached for a sword. As he advanced towards Paris, a voice from the crowd begged him to stop. The old shepherd appeared, knelt in front of Priam and explained that this unknown boy was actually his long-lost son. Priam, who had never lost the guilt he felt for condemning his son to death, was delighted. Ignoring the prophecy of Paris's birth, he welcomed the handsome youth into his family. He no longer feared what fate had foretold – that this son would cause the destruction of his city.

ABOVE *A Greek bronze head of the goddess of love, Aphrodite, who promised the most beautiful woman in the world – Helen of Sparta – to Paris.*

PARIS GOES TO SPARTA

Some time after he returned to Troy, Priam sent Paris to the city of Sparta as the leader of a peaceful delegation. It was not uncommon for the son of a king to lead a delegation of that sort. It was, of course, expected that the members of the foreign group should behave with the very best of good manners. It was here that Aphrodite's promise was to be fulfilled. Paris was an honoured guest of the city's king, Menelaus. He was liked by his host, as he was handsome, well mannered, polite and eager to please. Spartan men and women marvelled at his skill as a runner when he took part in games.

One woman watched him eagerly above all others: Helen, the wife of Menelaus. She had been told by her husband to treat the young man well. So taken with Paris was the Spartan king, that he likened him to a son. However, Paris was not behaving with any filial loyalty.

Courtiers watched as Paris whispered to Helen, bestowed gifts upon her, fed her from his own plate and drank from her bowl. Eventually these loyal subjects

HELEN

"Was this the face that launched a thousand ships,

And burnt the topless towers of Ilium?"

Christopher Marlowe – Doctor Faustus

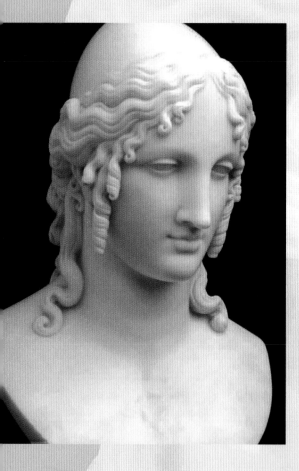

Her birth was a wonder, born from an egg laid by Leda (or Nemesis in some versions of the myth), Helen's father was Zeus, who came to her mother disguised as a swan. Even at the age of twelve, she was lovely enough to attract the attention of Theseus of Athens, who kidnapped her, determined to marry a daughter of Zeus. However, Helen was rescued by her brothers, Castor and Polydeuces.

Many mortals wished to marry the lovely Helen, among them Odysseus and Ajax. Finally she agreed to marry Menelaus, King of Sparta. Her failed suitors agreed that should Helen betray her husband, then they would band together to support him. So when Helen took flight with Paris the war against Troy was inevitable.

Many hated her because her beauty brought suffering to so many. In his play *Helen*, Euripides gives her the following line:

"Many a life beside Scamander's streams perished for me."

And in Hecuba he described how many Trojans felt about her:

"For grief I fainted, cursing Helen the sister of Castor and Polydeuces. I cursed Paris the shepherd from Mount Ida. It was their marriage, which was not a marriage but misery sent by some evil Fate, that robbed me of my country and threw me from my home…"

SPARTA AND ITS WARRIORS

Sparta, a city state in the middle of what is today called the Peloponnese, was fiercely independent. Ruled by a military elite it was not a city of culture like Athens. Young boys were installed in barracks at an early age where they were rigorously trained in military skills. In battle the young warriors were frequently paired with fellow soldiers, often their lovers, as it was believed that they would fight more fiercely to protect their partner. This was a society that thrived on war. Any child that was born sickly or deformed was immediately taken from its mother and left to die on the hills around the city. The Spartan culture was such that strength and heroic bravery were paramount.

Kings of Sparta also commanded the army. Long after the Trojan War had ended, and even in Homer's time, Spartans were still regarded as the toughest of warriors. In 480BC, in an act of spectacular courage, the Spartan leader Leonidas took 299 of his men to Thermopylae, as a vast Persian army advanced on Greece. He vowed to hold the pass to allow time for his coalition army of seven thousand men to retreat and warn the other Greeks of the advancing Persians. Leonidas's men held the pass until every single one of them had been slain by the Persians.

summoned up the courage to warn Menelaus of the behaviour of Paris and Helen. However, the king refused to believe that the leader of a delegation from another ruler would behave dishonourably.

The gods looked down as the two young people whispered and touched hands and gazed into each other's eyes. Some of the gods were troubled and others were amused. Had Aphrodite blinded Paris with love? She certainly favoured this young Trojan.

Menelaus was called to Crete for his grandfather's funeral. On the day that he left, Helen and Paris sailed for Troy. When Menelaus heard the news he sent out a rallying call to his friends and allies and the Greeks came to his aid.

In Troy Helen was feted and Paris vowed she would never be returned to her husband. Only his brother, the brave Hector, known as "the horse tamer" and a noble and a powerful warrior, did not fall under the spell of Helen's beauty. Hector's wife Andromache was as wary as her husband.

Paris had broken the sacred customs that bind a guest to behave honourably towards his host. Only Helen's beauty prevented the Trojans sending her back to her husband.

THE GREEK FLEET

So the Greeks heard the call of Menelaus and came to his aid as they had promised. They sailed for Troy. Their ships sailed to the city carrying warriors, princes and kings from Sparta, from Corinth, from Mycenae, from Sicyon, from Halkidiki and from Ithaca. From Samos and Thassos they came. They sailed from Paphos and from Cos, and from Igouminitsa in Corfu. Epidaurus gave warriors and they came from Mantinea and Crete.

Among the warriors were Idomeneus, the spearman, and Odysseus, the fox, who left behind his faithful wife, Penelope. Diomedes, the brave, sailed with eighty ships; Ajax came from Salamis with twelve ships; Nestor, a wise old man, brought a crew eager to hear the crash of bronze on bronze. Dressed in gold armour Nastes came to war and the great Achilles came too with fifty black-prowed, black-sailed, open ships each containing fifty warriors.

The ships came, swan prowed, crashing through the dark green sea and over sparkling dawn waves. They rode at anchor in the night, swooping like carrion birds through the crashing spray close to the black cliffs.

A thousand ships came to Troy to avenge the wrong done to the King of Sparta. They gathered under the leadership of their High King, Agamemnon, brother of Menelaus. Ten thousand and more men came. The Greeks hauled their ships on to the shores below the walls of Troy, where they set up camp to besiege the city. And the Gods looked down from Olympus, choosing their favourites and deciding who to support in the war that they knew was about to erupt.

SHIPS

Homer writes of fast wooden boats that are long, low and narrow with just the minimal amount of decking where men could stow their tents and other gear. He describes them as "high prowed, swift, hollow, sea riding, black painted, scarlet prowed". In *The Odyssey* boats are described as being made from many types of wood, oak and pine being especially sought after. The simple boats were built along a keel that came above the waterline in elegant curves. The hull was usually painted black and fixed in place either using tenon joints or wooden dowels. These were ships for coasting, not for crossing wide open oceans. Men would not usually sleep on board these ships but drew the vessels up onto beaches and slept alongside them.

Small boats, with ten oars on each side, were used for exploration, to carry supplies or for the rapid movement of a small number of men. A boat with fifty oars – twenty-five on each side – was used for ferrying warriors. The oars were held in place by leather straps along both sides of the hull. A steering oar at the stern was manipulated by one man who stood on a small platform above the deck. Each oar was worked by a single man sitting on a bench that crossed from one side of the open boat to the other. The benches gave added strength to the structure.

The ships sometimes had a simple sail made of many linen squares that had been sewn together. It was raised on a single cross beam with ropes (sheets) to attach it to the hull of the ship. The sail and mast would be temporary and easily removed.

These simple ships were not necessarily those in use when *The Iliad* was written down. Homer may well have used the images he found on vases and painted friezes, which were already old when he saw them, to describe his ships.

RIGHT *A watercolour of a Greek warship. Ships like this carried fifty oarsmen and are of the type that Homer would have been familiar with.*

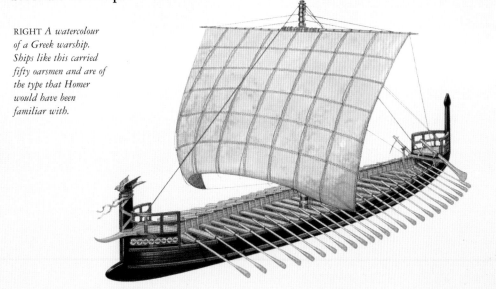

CHAPTER FOUR

SCHLIEMANN'S DREAM BEGINS

They ran beneath the walls of Troy. Hector and the murderous Achilles. They went past the curving walls and a long fig tree, along a rough track. They came to the two springs that are the source of the Scamander which flowed across the plain. One spring is cold and the other hot and steaming even in winter. Close by are the stone troughs where women washed their clothes before the days of war…

The Iliad, Book XXII

This is how Homer describes the beginning of the murderous chase of Hector by Achilles towards the end of *The Iliad*. It is this description that Heinrich Schliemann was to use to discover the true site of the lost city of Troy.

SCHLIEMANN IN ITHACA

In April 1868 Schliemann set off to discover the palace of Odysseus on the island of Ithaca. He stopped in Corfu on the way and wrote in his journal that the writings of Homer provided absolute proof that this was the island of the Phaecians, where Odysseus was shipwrecked on his way back to Ithaca. He claimed that a large stream called the Fountain of Cressida was the place where Nausicaa washed the laundry with her maids and met Odysseus.

Schliemann was determined to use *The Iliad* and also *The Odyssey* as if they were guidebooks. He described how he walked beside the river, often up to his chest in water and mud from irrigation canals and flooded fields. After walking for half an hour he saw two large cut stones close to the mouth of the river. These stones were the basins in which the Corfiots washed their sheets and clothes. Schliemann was certain that he had found the place where, according to Homer, Odysseus had landed on his way home from the ten-year siege of Troy. He claimed that this must be where Nausicaa came because, again according to Homer, after she and her maids had washed the laundry

OPPOSITE *The plains of Troy looking towards the hillside.*

RIGHT *The archaeologist Heinrich Schliemann whose dream was to discover the true location of the lost city of Troy.*

they spread it out to dry on the pebble beach along the seashore. They then bathed and played, waking Odysseus who was asleep in the bushes. Schliemann believed that this was all the proof he needed, and that in the space of a half-hour walk, he had discovered the site where Odysseus had rested. This was a man who leapt to conclusions that suited his theories on the slightest of evidence.

Schliemann travelled on by boat to Ithaca where Odysseus had lived with Penelope, according to tradition. Everything he seemed to observe provided proof for his theories. He describes a discovery on the peak of Mount Aetos, where, with a team of four workers, he cleared a site where he claimed the olive tree from which Odysseus made his marriage bed had grown.

He left his workers digging and moved to another flat area where he

ODYSSEUS

Son of Laertes, ruler of the island of Ithaca, Odysseus was one of the first suitors of Helen (see p.20). When she married Menelaus, Odysseus, a cunning man, suggested that all the other men who had wanted to marry her should band together to support Menelaus if anything went wrong with the marriage.

When the moment came to stand by his sacred oath, Odysseus pretended to be mad, as it had been revealed to him in a prophecy that should he go to war, he would not return for twenty years. Dressed as a madman, he was found by Palamedes, ploughing his land and planting salt. His duplicity was revealed when Palamedes placed Odysseus's baby son, Telemachus, in front of the plough. Odysseus avoided the child, proving he was of reasonable mind. He was compelled to join Menelaus's army.

Once at war he proved to be a shrewd and wise general. He was also brave, venturing behind enemy lines with Diomedes to spy on the Trojans and, incidentally, to steal some fine horses for himself. In some versions of the Greek myths the idea of the Wooden Horse, which defeated the Trojans and led to the destruction of the city, is Odysseus's idea.

His long journey home is the subject of Homer's other great epic, *The Odyssey*, in which the hero, accompanied by twelve ships and their men, faces many amazing adventures. At the end of the ten-year journey, the only survivor was Odysseus himself. Disguised, he arrived home to Ithaca to discover that his wife Penelope had been besieged by suitors whom she had refused. Moved by her fidelity, Odysseus slaughtered the suitors with the help of Laertes and Telemachus.

LEFT *Odysseus, King of Ithaca, captained a boat such as the one depicted on this vase when he joined the fleet going to besiege Troy.*

began to dig. There he discovered a small but beautiful vase, which he smashed with his pick axe, only to discover that it was filled with human ashes. He found more vases on the site and broke most of them trying to get them out with utterly unsuitable tools. This was something he continued to do throughout his archaeological expeditions. These were the days when spades and picks were used rather than trowels and soft brushes, and Schliemann was the least meticulous archaeologist. Nevertheless, he declared that it was quite possible that the ashes he had discovered were those of Odysseus, his wife Penelope and their descendants. How he could make this conjecture is impossible to tell. He may have believed what he claimed, but he had no real proof.

Schliemann was not interested in recording his discoveries, or using any of the simple systems in use at that time, which ensured that each item found was related to its position on the site. Schliemann was after sensation and fame – as for his claim that the ashes were those of Odysseus, there was no other evidence, it was merely speculation. This method of work and of leaping to conclusions was typical of the way he continued to work as an archaeologist.

Even when attacked by a farmer's dogs Schliemann was influenced by Homer's words, remembering what the desperate Odysseus did in similar circumstances. Odysseus sat down and dropped his walking stick. Schliemann did the same as the snarling dogs came closer. The dogs circled around him until their owner, a farmer, arrived. The German berated the man for having such fierce and savage dogs. Schliemann claimed that the farmer said that his father and grandfather descended as far back as Odysseus, and had always kept dogs like this so it was also his right to do so. Folk memory may lie close to the surface, but Schliemann is surely gilding the lily here.

ABOVE The view towards the Dardanelles. Note how few trees are found on the windy plains.

TO TROY

Schliemann left the island of Ithaca and took a passage to the Dardanelles and the hill called Hissarlik. On August 8, 1868 he came on horseback onto the river plain that was to be the site of his greatest discovery. Tradition had it that a small village called Bunarbashi was the site of Troy. Other archaeologists and scholars had declared that this village might be the site of the "mighty walls of Ilium [the Latin name for Troy]". It was not a village that impressed Schliemann. He described it with some reserve.

Even as he came closer to realizing his dream, Schliemann had time to count birds' nests and the number of inhabitants in the area. Bunarbashi was a filthy village consisting of twenty-three hovels, and was populated by a mixture of Turks and Albanians. Every house had up to a dozen stork's nests on its flat roof. Schliemann discovered that the birds were useful because they killed vipers and the noisy frogs that infested the local marshland.

He hired a Greek-speaking Albanian as a guide, and agreed to stay the night in his interpreter's home. When he went inside the house he discovered that bedbugs swarmed up the walls, over the floors and on the bench that his host offered him as a

bed. However tough Schliemann was, he could not face sleeping in such a filthy place. When he asked for a drink he was given milk into a bowl that he claimed had never been washed. He declared that he would rather die than touch it. He chose to spend the night in the open air instead.

Schliemann may have been a rogue and someone who could mould evidence to suit his own theories, but he was willing to suffer for his dream. He spent some days casting about the vast plain and he was not convinced. Eminent archaeologists may have declared Bunarbashi to be the site of Troy, but as far as Schliemann was concerned it did not coincide with his guidebook. And *The Iliad* was surely correct. Though inexperienced, he proclaimed that other archaeologists were wrong. His letters and journals fail to record that other scholars before him had already decided that Bunarbashi was not the site of Troy. The debate had begun when a French antiquarian called Lechevalier declared for Bunarbashi, and a General von Moltke announced that he believed it was the only possible site for the fortress.

Then Charles Maclaren, the editor of the *Scotsman*, claimed that Hissarlik was the actual site. The archaeology began with the bitter squabbles that seem to characterize the world of the archaeologist and the ancient historian. A gentler voice came from Frank Calvert, the American Vice Consul at Canakkale. He had long believed Hissarlik was the site of Troy, and had already done some preliminary work on the half of the hill that he had purchased from the Turks. Indeed he had uncovered a temple to Minerva on the site in the mid-1860s.

Clearly the idea of Hissarlik as Troy was never uniquely Schliemann's, yet he was careful never to say as much. He refused to share credit with anyone over anything.

FRANK CALVERT

A good amateur archaeologist, Frank Calvert was devoted to the works of Homer. He and his brothers were Anglo-Levantine merchants and land-owners who understood the mindset of the Turkish officials they dealt with. They acted as consuls for Prussia and Britain in Rhodes, the Dardanelles and the area including Hissarlik.

SCHLIEMANN'S DREAM BEGINS

Calvert had bought land from local owners with the aim of undergoing an archaeological dig in search of Troy. He discovered walls constructed of cut stone standing out of the hillside, which he believed were more recent than those of the heroic city of Troy. This meant to him that the city described by Homer had to be buried under the remains of later cities on the site.

He announced his findings in a paper to the London Archaeological Institute in 1864 – four years before Schliemann arrived in the area. Calvert was a gentleman and an amateur with a trusting manner. He was very much a scholar eager to share knowledge. This was never going to be Schliemann's way – he was determined that he would be the one to find Troy and the treasures he was sure would lie in the city.

Schliemann brought to the search the instinct of a truffle hound on the scent. It would prove successful in one way and a disaster for the more methodical, scholarly approach. His hunger for fame, adulation and academic recognition drove him. Initially, Schliemann found it convenient to cooperate with the Englishman. It was not in Calvert's nature to be competitive about such things, but he was to find the German's vanity and his disregard of any point of view other than his own irritating at first and finally insupportable. He was ill prepared for Schliemann's ruthlessness.

SCHLIEMANN AT HISSARLIK

Schliemann walked along the banks of the Kara Menderes, looking at other possible sites. He tried to make them fit the description of the chase around the city in which Achilles pursued Hector three times round the walls looking for vengeance. Alternatively he tried to find the place from which Zeus might have looked down on the city from Mount Ida. If Homer had described these scenes, they must have been real, and the only possible conclusion was that Hissarlik was the place.

Schliemann hired men from Bunarbashi to dig trenches on various sites. He found nothing. Then he walked with five men across the malarial swamps on the plain; according to Homer such swamps came close to the walls of the city. Schliemann climbed to the top of the hill and found it covered in potsherds (shards of pottery) and worked blocks of marble. Four marble pillars seemed to indicate the site of a temple. He believed he was already on the site of a large and once flourishing city, and that he was standing on top of the hill that concealed the site of ancient Ilium. Schliemann believed that Hissarlik was indeed the site of Troy.

It is true that from the other side of the hill it is possible to see the mountain range that includes Mount Ida. According to Schliemann there was no possible room for doubt: beneath him was the Troy of Priam and his sons. Schliemann was convinced that all he had to do was dig. He applied for permission from the authorities. It was near the end of the season and almost too late to begin, so he decided to spend the time in hand arranging labour and gathering the tools needed for such a vast undertaking. The hill had waited for three thousand years. It could wait another year for his attention.

Schliemann wrote to Calvert from Paris asking for his advice about what he might need and then attending to more personal matters. He did not know then that he would be thwarted by a higher authority, just as his hero Achilles was thwarted by the High King Agamemnon.

CHAPTER FIVE

A TERRIBLE QUARREL

The Iliad is set in the tenth year of the Greek siege of Troy. The epic begins with a huge quarrel that ignites the catastrophic anger of the great Greek hero, Achilles, and sets in motion the chain of events that leads to the destruction of the besieged city.

From time to time during the lengthy siege a Greek ship and its crew would slip away to raid the nearby coast, returning to their camp with the fruits of their plunder. On one such raid, Agamemnon took as his prisoner a girl called Chryseis. Achilles accompanied the High King on the raid, returning with a lovely girl named Briseis, who was a prize for his courage.

During a pause in the fighting, Agamemnon rested in his quarters of the Greek camp. He was eating with his generals and the talk was of home, of children they missed and of other adventures they had had. Into the glimmer of the fire stepped an old man. Followed by two servants pulling a cart, he walked past Agamemnon's guards and towards his table. On his back he carried a shepherd's bag and in his hand was a staff on which was an insignia that identified him as priest of the god Apollo.

AGAMEMNON

The son of Atreus and the brother of Menelaus, Agamemnon was supreme leader of the forces that besieged Troy. He had undisputed power over all the assembled Greek leaders and their warriors.

Agamemnon was boastful, greedy and ruthless. When the Greek fleet was becalmed near Aulis on its way to Troy, he called on Calchas, his seer, to discover why the gods were against him. The seer revealed that Artemis, the goddess of hunting, was angry because Agamemnon had boasted that of the two, he was the better hunter. Calchas told Agamemnon and those with him that unless he sacrificed his daughter, Iphigenia, they would be forever becalmed. The High King agreed to sacrifice his daughter and, in Homer's version of the tale, she was saved from the bronze blade when Artemis substituted a deer on the altar and spirited the girl away. In other versions of the myth, she is sacrificed for the Greek fleet.

Agamemnon offended Achilles with his greed and ruthless use of power, and his stubborn pride nearly caused the defeat of the Greeks. After the siege of Troy, Agamemnon returned home with Cassandra, daughter of Priam, whom he had taken as a concubine. Once home his wife Clytemnestra and her lover, Aegisthus, murdered the king and his mistress.

LEFT *Agamemnon,*
High King and leader
of the Mycenaean Greek
army that besieged Troy.

OPPOSITE *A wall*
painting from Pompeii
shows Patroclus
separating Briseis from
the hero Achilles.

The old man stopped just inside the circle of light cast by the flares around the camp and waited. The soldiers who had watched him arrive were impressed by his quiet dignity and the sadness of his face. Eventually, Agamemnon looked across at him and asked his name. The old man replied:

"I am Chryses, priest of Apollo and father of Chryseis whom you took when you sacked our land down the coast. I want my daughter back. I don't expect you to give her to her father therefore I have brought a ransom."

Chryses turned and took the covers off the wagon that his two servants had brought. In it was a treasure of bronze pots, swords, lances, a shield of fine work, vases, and ewers inlaid with gold – a king's ransom for his beloved daughter.

Agamemnon looked the old man up and down as he chewed on a meat bone. The old man looked quietly into the High King's eyes. He seemed to have no fear. Around them the conversation died away. Then Agamemnon threw the bone to the two war dogs he kept near him at all times, and refused the old man's request.

"You can get off out of my sight and out of this camp. I never want to see you again. I will take your daughter, Chryseis to my palace and she will be a servant to me and shall be taken to my bed whenever I want her. And if I see you again I shall feed you to my dogs as I feed meat. Take your ransom and go."

The king's men were unhappy at the way he spoke to this grieving old man and priest of Apollo. For a moment Chryses hesitated, then he turned slowly and walked through the ranks of soldiers. They made way for him – here was a brave man who deserved respect. Achilles said what the men only dared to think.

"That was not worthy of a High King. He was a father sorrowing for his child. A brave man despite his grey hairs. You were wrong to treat him so cruelly."

Still Agamemnon refused to release the girl. There was murmuring and much disquiet among the Greeks.

The old man walked quietly along the shore. The waves lapped softly at the sand and over his sandled feet. As he walked he prayed to the god Apollo, the archer. Apollo heard him and was angry that his priest had been so badly treated. He shot an arrow from his bow, bringing plague upon the men. The next morning many soldiers were found to have died and guards were discovered dead at their posts. This pestilence stayed for many days.

BELOW *Apollo, the god of healing, prophecy and the arts, whose priest Chryses was insulted by Agamemnon. Apollo was furious and punished the Greek army with a plague.*

CALCHAS

"What is a seer? A man who, with luck tells the truth sometimes, with frequent lies, but when his luck runs out, collapses then and there!"

Achilles to Clytemnestra in Euripides's *Iphigenia in Aulis*

Calchas came from a family of seers. He was taken by Agamemnon from his home in Megara to accompany the Greeks to war. At Aulis, Calchas saw a snake climb a tree and eat ten fledglings in a nest. From this he divined that the war would last ten years.

When the Greek fleet was becalmed at Aulis on its way to Troy, Calchas suggested that the fleet would only escape the quiet sea if Iphigenia were sacrificed. It was also he who explained why Apollo was slaughtering the army with the plague, an episode described by Homer at the beginning of *The Iliad*.

Calchas travelled home after the siege ended, where he met another seer. It had been prophesied that when Calchas met a superior seer that he would die. It seems that Mopsus was that man. He answered what Calchas believed was an impossible question correctly. Calchas shut his eyes and died on the spot. Some say he died of anger, others say he died from grief.

Achilles asked Calchas, a seer, to make sacrifice and to divine the cause. Calchas cut the throat of a bull on the seashore, made offerings to the gods and discovered the reason. He begged Achilles to tell Agamemnon but Achilles told him he, Calchas, had to tell the king himself. He promised he would protect the seer from the anger of the king.

A delegation went to the tent where Agamemnon lay. Calchas told him that the mighty Apollo was firing his arrows to bring plague into the camp, and that he would go on doing so until the girl was sent back to her father. By treating Chryses so rudely, he had insulted Apollo. Agamemnon found Calchas's prophecies tiresome.

"You have never foretold anything but evil. You love to prophesy evil. I have never heard a word of good from you… Nor has anything good come about as a result of your prophecies."

Agamemnon still refused to release the girl. Then, some in his camp, including Achilles, made it clear that unless he did what was asked, they would take their ships to sea and head for home to escape the anger of Apollo. So Agamemnon reluctantly agreed and the girl Chryseis was taken back to her father by Odysseus.

THE WRATH OF ACHILLES

Agamemnon, who was mean spirited and angry, wanted something in return for Chryseis. He sent two soldiers to bring Briseis, the favourite of Achilles, to his tent. It was the will of the king, and Achilles could not oppose that will. But this great soldier could refuse to fight. The furious Achilles spoke to his mother, Thetis of the silver feet, asking her to help him with his plight.

Thetis flew from the sea to Mount Olympus, knelt before the mighty Zeus and asked that her son's dishonour be punished. She asked him to ensure that her son, who was fated to die before his comrades, had his honour restored to him and with that, Briseis, the girl. Thetis asked that Troy should appear to be winning the battle. Zeus said nothing. She held his knees and begged him again. Zeus knew that if he agreed to Thetis's request he would have trouble from Hera, his wife.

"She is forever complaining that I favour the Trojans and she is jealous of you

RIGHT *This painting by Peter Paul Rubens shows Thetis dipping her son Achilles into the River Styx.*

Thetis. So, I promise to do what you ask but leave Olympus and get back to the sea before she sees you talking to me."

However, Hera did see Thetis and demanded to know what Zeus had promised. The great god refused to tell her but she already knew that he had agreed that the Greeks should be pushed back almost into their ships by the Trojans. If this happened, Agamemnon would surely beg Achilles to fight and then, and only then, would there be any chance that the Greek hero would join the battle. Hera was not pleased.

On the plain the men gathered themselves to fight again. Behind the Greeks the stunted willow trees that grew along the River Scamander bore strange fruit. The black carrion crows perched in the branches and waited and watched for the first of the dead to be dragged clear of the battle. They would feast well today.

Achilles leaned against his boat, heard the preparations for battle and closed his eyes. He had lost Briseis, his prize, and she had pleased him. Achilles would not fight because he had been robbed of a woman. Three thousand years later, Heinrich Schliemann also had women on his mind.

ACHILLES

The mother of Achilles, Thetis, silver-footed goddess of the sea, was wooed by both Zeus and Poseidon. However, the gods abandoned their courtship when warned by the oracle Prometheus that any child born of Thetis would be greater than his father. So Thetis was encouraged to marry a mortal, Peleus.

Thetis was greatly respected by the other gods. When Achilles was born she already knew that he was going to be a great warrior but she was determined that he would be protected from death. She took her baby under the Earth to the Styx, the river in Greek myth that all men and women had to cross when they die. She knew that if she bathed him in the roaring waters, he would be safe from any danger of death from men in battle. Thetis held him by the heel and dipped him into the black, foaming waters, granting him immortality. However, the one spot that was not immersed, his heel, remained his weak spot.

By the time of the abduction of Helen, Achilles was a grown man. He was able to run faster than a fighting leopard, was as brave a fighter as a wild boar and as cunning as any fox in battle. The warriors sometimes called him Achilles "of the bright armour" and he rallied to the cause of Menelaus because he and his followers, the wolf wild men of the Halkidiki, lived to fight. They were called the Myrmidons and were implacable in the killing fields.

CHAPTER SIX

THE FIRST DIG

Wintering in Paris in 1868, Heinrich Schliemann began to consider marriage.

His previous experience of wedlock had been unhappy.

Schliemann's Russian wife, who had never been compliant, had flatly refused to divorce him. As a result, he was compelled to travel to America to cut his ties with her. Now, however, Heinrich Schliemann felt the need for a new companion.

The vibrant French capital threw many temptations in the way of a rich, unmarried bachelor. A Parisian wife would have been an easy catch for Schliemann, but he had decided that such women were not for him. He was concerned, he wrote, about their morals. This self-made man was not going to squander the money he had made on an extravagant, dissolute and fashionable lifestyle. Despite almost constant pain in his ears, from which he suffered for most of his life, Schliemann maintained a healthy regime that he was determined to stick to.

Obsessed as he was by Greece and all things Greek, he was determined to marry a woman from the country he loved. Schliemann asked a friend in Athens to find him a suitable candidate. He demanded that she need not be wealthy but she had to be intelligent and willing to learn. She must, he wrote, "be enthusiastic about Homer and the rebirth of my beloved Greece". His friend sent him some photographs, among them was an image of a dark beauty named Sophia Engastromenos. Schliemann decided that she was the one for him. She was no more than a schoolgirl; Schliemann was forty-six.

OPPOSITE *The huts in which the newly married Schliemann lived with his wife on the hill of Hissarlik.*

BELOW *A portrait of Schliemann and his young wife, Sophia shortly after their marriage.*

Sophia was the daughter of Cretan parents. Her father had fought with distinction in the Greek War of Independence in the 1820s and was now a modest draper. Schliemann wrote to the girl's father to tell him that he would only marry Sophia if she had a desire to learn. He believed, he wrote, that a beautiful young girl could only respect and love an old man if she had an enthusiasm for knowledge in which he was more advanced than she.

Casting aside some initial doubts, Schliemann travelled to Athens, where he met Sophia and agreed to the extremely avaricious terms and conditions her parents proposed. They were determined that this rich foreigner was not going to catch their lovely daughter for nothing, and they would go on squeezing him for money for many years to come. Schliemann asked the girl why she had agreed to marry a man old enough to be her father; she replied candidly that it was because he was rich. He was shocked by this honest response, but the marriage took place and, against the odds perhaps, it was successful.

Sophia's life was transformed the instant they wed. She had married a very rich man and she took her role as companion, wife and, eventually, mother very seriously. It was she who smoothed Schliemann's ruffled feathers when he felt he had been slighted by an academic institution that refused to take his work as an archaeologist or scholar seriously. She also worked as an overseer on her husband's digs and colluded in his thefts from the sites. Sophia did not spare herself and her husband admired her for it. She was the perfect partner for this difficult, impatient and unforgiving man. Just before his death he wrote:

Words fail me to celebrate our marriage. At all times you were to me a loving wife, a good comrade and a dependable guide in difficult situations, as well as a dear companion of the road and a mother second to none... Therefore today I promise that I shall marry you again in a future life.

LOSING PATIENCE

Life, even at the beginning of their marriage, was not going to prove easy for the couple. When the digging season began in 1870 Schliemann came to Hissarlik alone. He had not yet received his firman – the set of papers containing permission from the Turkish authorities to begin the dig. Without this, his search for Troy could not begin.

The Turkish authorities were not going to be rushed. Schliemann knew these papers were vital, but he did not understand that it served no purpose to lose patience, to shout or to try to use the authority of the American Consul to influence officials. He needed Sophia with him to calm him down and to explain how things worked in the Ottoman Empire, but she was in Athens.

Schliemann had not come to Hissarlik to stand and do nothing. Ignoring the advice of Frank Calvert, he saw no reason to wait for the *firman* to arrive. He hired men from the surrounding villages and began to dig. As he did so, Schliemann found a vase containing ashes, bronze nails, shards of pottery and a terracotta bust that he immediately claimed represented Helen of Troy.

Permission still did not come. Calvert urged caution, but patience was not something Schliemann understood. If bureaucrats wanted to stand in his way, he believed he could just brush them aside. He could not understand the hostility of the Turkish officials, and he also did not see that

LEFT *This nineteenth-century photograph shows Turkish men in traditional dress – Schliemann often became frustrated with Turkish customs.*

his attitude was no help. He never wanted to hear anything that countered what he wanted to believe. The delays and excuses infuriated him. With his small, unsmiling eyes and large moustache, Schliemann did not cut an heroic figure with the Turkish authorities and they made this pushy, impatient, rude and angry German businessman wait.

Aware that he was acting illegally, the locals who were digging for him blackmailed Schliemann into agreeing that they could remove any suitable building materials they uncovered. They carted off blocks of cut stone to add new walls to their houses or to build walls and animal pens on the surrounding plains. The workers returned with demands for more payment and they refused his offer to buy the land. Appalled at the blackmail, Schliemann dismissed the workers.

Schliemann's vision possessed him. Hissarlik was a modest hill but would require a huge amount of excavation if he was to dig down into Homer's Troy. He knew that to get to the city of Priam and his sons, he had to remove all the layers of cut stones, rubble and earth that made up the hill. He was determined to complete this as quickly and ruthlessly as he could. He believed that beneath the hilltop lay the huge gates of Troy, temples dedicated to Athena and Apollo, magnificent palaces and wide, paved streets. Above all, Schliemann intended to prove wrong the hostile academics who had mocked his belief that *The Iliad* would guide him. He was convinced that he had discovered the site of Homer's Troy.

ABOVE *Schliemann believed that the ruins and the earth covering the hillside at Hissarlik contained buried temples dedicated to gods such as Apollo (above), the huge gates of Troy and the palace of Priam.*

Hadn't other visionaries come before him? Hadn't Alexander the Great visited the temple in Troy before he set off on his conquest of the world? The same Alexander who believed he descended from Achilles, himself descended from the gods. Alexander had taken the armour hanging in the temple to Athena at Troy, which was said to be the armour of his heroic ancestor. At the age of twenty-four Alexander had conquered his world. Maybe a businessman nearing fifty could conquer his. But it would not happen if he obeyed the rules and waited for permission.

Schliemann wrote to scholarly journals in France and Germany, claiming that the subterranean walls that were emerging at Hissarlik were those of Priam's palace. In doing this, he made his illegal activities common knowledge. Cocking a snook at the Turkish authorities by boasting about his discoveries in print was stupid, but this supremely arrogant individual saw no reason not to do it.

Frank Calvert was appalled that Schliemann had boasted of digging at Hissarlik without permission. Worse still, he had even boasted about removing items from the site. He wrote to Schliemann telling him, in no uncertain terms, how foolish he thought these actions had been. Calvert was concerned that the effects of Schliemann's actions might be felt by other, more honest, archaeologists digging in Turkey. He was convinced it had only been a matter of time before the *firman* arrived, however, Schliemann had made the authorities lose face.

But Schliemann never understood that playing fair, being patient and restraining from boasting were more likely to achieve the desired results than acting hastily and hectoring the Turkish officials. His illegal actions had put him at risk of being ordered off the site.

Back in Athens Sophia gave birth to a daughter in May 1871. In August Schliemann was in London when the *firman* was finally granted. It was late in the digging season, but he went to Athens and from there to Hissarlik. By now it was October and the digging season was almost over.

PERMISSION GRANTED

The terms of the agreement meant that Schliemann had to promise to turn over half of all his discoveries to the Turkish authorities, though he was allowed to keep the other half. All uncovered ruins were to be left untouched and he had to pay for all the work done. Schliemann promised to obey these conditions. His digs at Hissarlik over the next few years would show what his promises were worth.

In that first short season Schliemann used a team of men to cut a trench across the site, which eventually went right through the mound. He was determined to dig down as far as the bedrock. It was a method that would result in the demolition of many ancient buildings and artefacts. However, this suited his attitude: if what was uncovered did not fit the period of Priam's Troy, it was of no interest to Schliemann.

He used picks and shovels and removed barrow loads of material from the trench. There was no measurement and no proper assessment of what was being destroyed. One historical level was often mixed up with another. Pots, figurines, axe heads, bowls and blades were scattered or shattered by such crude methods. Such a cavalier attitude towards potentially precious artefacts seems odd, as Schliemann was one of the first to understand that the style of a piece of pottery could fix its date more accurately than any other method available at the time. But the pursuit of Priam's Troy was everything to this man; anything else that was discovered simply got in the way.

Schliemann arrived at the site each morning and demanded that the workers dig faster. Few breaks were allowed – they were paid to dig, and dig they would. The trench sliced through one archaeological level after another. Schliemann continued to write articles and letters to journals and newspapers all over the world bragging about his actions. Many of the scholars he contacted thought he was just a pushy businessman dabbling in an area of which he had no real knowledge. One appalled scholar, who represented the attitudes of many, claimed that the dig was "rape not archaeology".

But Schliemann had no interest in the opinions of those who criticized him. He confessed that some of the objects he found, such as round objects with holes in the centre resembling spinning tops, puzzled him. He asked other archaeologists what they were but he didn't wait for answers, continuing to slice ever deeper through the earth and destroying anything in his way. Eventually, Schliemann's workers came to a building that lay across the line of the trench. It was nearly 60 feet (20m) long and 40 feet (13m) wide, and clearly something significant. However, it was too recent to be anything associated with Priam's Troy. So the workmen destroyed it.

He went on to discover metal objects and fine pottery, as well as some owl-headed vases. The owl was a creature sacred to the goddess Athena, a deity that Schliemann believed was sacred to Troy – he was getting close. He continued to boast in academic circles about his successes and wrote that it would not be long before he unearthed the real city of Troy, home of "the long haired Helen".

RIGHT *Schliemann showed some of his finds at the Society of Antiquaries at South Kensington in 1878.*

As autumn drew in, Schliemann stopped the dig and returned to Athens to join his wife, to write his journals and to confront his critics. He complained in letters and articles that his academic critics never seemed to be able to forgive him for solving the greatest mystery of the ancient world without the necessary credentials. They were, he crowed, jealous that a self-made man could bring his fortune and his great organizational skills to the enterprise of proving that the city of Troy – the city of Homer's epic – existed.

The gods may have looked down from Mount Olympus in disbelief, but they did little to punish this arrogant would-be scholar. Then again, the gods were used to duplicity and arrogance and perhaps this vain, short, red-faced man amused them with his antics on Hissarlik. But who were these gods?

CHAPTER SEVEN

THE GODS OF OLYMPUS

In Ancient Greece, deities such as Zeus, Apollo, Hermes and Aphrodite appeared to be "real", even to the most intelligent and educated people. Unlike mere mortals these gods and goddesses were all-powerful. They lived according to their own codes of conduct, which were sometimes broken, and they had arguments and forged alliances just as mortals did.

The gods of Ancient Greece lived on Mount Olympus. Zeus, "the thunder maker", was senior in the immortal hierarchy, although there were times when individual gods defied him. The deities moved among mortals disguised as elements, animals or other humans. They had the ability to interfere in battles and duels; they could create new life and procreate with ordinary mortals; if they desired, they could protect a favoured human and they could also bestow bad luck on those they disliked. Heroic men claimed kinship with the gods, something that would not have seemed unlikely to those who listened to the epics told by Homer and his contemporaries, as it was believed that the gods were happy to spread their sexual favours among the brave and the beautiful.

WORSHIP AND CULTS

OPPOSITE *Mount Olympus, the mythical home of the Greek gods.*

BELOW *A bronze statue showing Zeus brandishing a thunderbolt. He was the most powerful of the Greek gods.*

In Homer's time each home had an altar and ritual and sacrifice to the gods was a part of day-to-day life. Worship was a personal matter between the supplicant and the god. For example, anyone setting out on a journey made an offering to the relevant god, just as a woman about to give birth prayed to a suitable goddess.

Priests made the major sacrifices, saw that festivals were celebrated, said prayers and observed the rites of each of the gods. For the goddesses there were priestesses, each schooled in the rites, needs and indeed, the expectations of their particular deity. Often these priests and priestesses were also men or women who had families to care for.

Because of this flexible attitude to the gods, men and women had no dogmatic rule or belief that theirs was the only way to worship. Alexander the Great continued this Greek tradition when he accepted and worshipped the gods of the countries he defeated. It was natural and also reasonable, in his view, to honour them. It would have been foolish and ill mannered to claim that the gods of the Persians or the Indians were inferior to those of his people.

The idea of sin was not something that concerned the Ancient Greeks. Men and women might make mistakes or be led into error by a god or a goddess. If an individual committed a personal offence against a god and felt guilty as a result, it was merely fate. The only way to combat such guilt was to be purified by the slighted deity, which required a ceremony in the presence of a priest or priestess versed in the practices of the cult of that god or goddess. The Greeks did not understand the concept of the sexual act being sinful in itself. If, however, such an act was done in order to exact revenge or to wilfully dishonour the victim blame would be attached to whoever had committed the act. According to the scholar E.V. Rieu, Homer

regards his gods though immortal as made in the image and likeness of man. With his deep respect for their almost unlimited powers and his aesthetic appreciation of their beauty, he betrays a very tolerant understanding of their motives and frailties. Homer never censures a god nor lets a mortal use a god's misdeeds as a pretext for his own.

In many ways the stories of the Trojan War are as much about the gods and goddesses of Olympus as they are about the heroes. They take sides, influence events and champion individuals, playing key roles in the epic tale.

ZEUS
The greatest of the Olympian gods was the mighty Zeus. He controlled the weather and the sky, and is often referred to as the "thunder maker", "cloud gatherer" or "rain maker". Zeus was seen as the life force. Essentially rational and ordered, he was the deity that humans, who regarded themselves as his children, followed as an example. Married first to Metis, he subsequently took as his wife, Hera, who may also have been his sister. Zeus had the habit of taking mortal women as lovers, often coming to them in disguise. For example, in some versions of the Greek myths, he visits Leda in the guise of a swan, a coupling that results in the birth of Helen. Other disguises used by Zeus to seduce mortal women included a bear and a white bull. In the matter of the siege of Troy, Zeus tried to be even handed.

BELOW *Athena, holding a shield on which is her symbol, the owl.*

ATHENA
Known as the "grey-eyed", Athena was a virgin goddess. She represented the hearth and feminine intuition, wisdom and was goddess of war. Her role gradually expanded until she became goddess and protector of cities — Athens is named for her.

Athena was born from the head of Zeus, who had swallowed her mother, Metis, whole. She was symbolized by an owl. Athena could be terrible in her vengeance if she was slighted in any way. When bathing in a stream, she was seen by Teiresias as he walked past. While gods were forever being seen naked, goddesses were not, and any human who saw a female deity in a state of undress risked a terrible fate. Athena's fury at Teiresias was such that "night seized the eyes of the youth", and she blinded him instantly. The mother of the youngster, who was bathing with the goddess, was appalled at such anger. Athena pitied her but pointed out that it was not she who had blinded the boy, but fate, which decreed that anyone who saw a goddess naked had to be punished. Relenting, she gave Teiresias the power to see into the future. Athena supported the Greeks, though the Trojans, not realizing this, worshipped her.

HEPHAESTUS

Sing, golden-voiced poet of Hephaestus famed for his craft.

With bright-eyed Athena he taught men glorious skills

Men who before lived in caves like wild animals

Have learned enough through Hephaestus to live in

    decent airy homes.

Hephaestus, give me success and prosperity

– Hymn to Hephaestus

The lame god, Hephaestus, has a name that may well mean "fire" in the antique language once spoken by the Greeks. The son of Zeus and Hera – though some sources say he was born of Hera alone – Hephaestus was a deity much loved by men for his power and his skill at making weapons. His ability to create objects of such great beauty meant that Hephaestus was also loved by women.

He made weapons for Athena and a sceptre for Agamemnon, but above all he liked to make gifts for Thetis, who ignored his crippled leg and was kind to him when his mother, ashamed of his deformity, banished Hephaestus from Olympus. At the request of Thetis, he forged a wonderful shield for her son, Achilles.

As decent and as kind as an Olympian god could be, Hephaestus was married to Aphrodite. He supported the Greeks in the Trojan War.

ARES
The bloody god of war and battle, Ares was the child of Zeus and Hera. He was disliked by the other deities on Olympus, who treated him with suspicion; he was also unpopular among mortals. Ares cuckolded Hephaestus in his own house. Homer writes of the way in which Hephaestus avenged himself. While Ares and Aphrodite made love, the crippled god fashioned an invisible net with which to trap the couple.

He fastened the netting to the bed and fixed it to a rafter over the bed. It was so finely made that it looked like a small cobweb. Then he left the room and went away. Ares crept into the house, took the goddess of love to bed and the netting dropped onto them. They were trapped in Hephaeston's net.

To humiliate them further, Hephaestus invited the other gods to view the trapped lovers. It was only when Poseidon pressurized Hephaestus that he released the embarrassed pair. Ares took the Trojan side in the war against the Greeks.

APHRODITE

Aphrodite comes in many disguises, but she is always associated with sensual love. The other goddesses were jealous of her because of her beauty and because she was able – and willing – to seduce the gods themselves. Aphrodite even managed to distract the mind of Zeus and send him chasing after mortal women.

To get his revenge, Zeus makes Aphrodite desire a mortal man. Homer wrote

Her veil was more dazzling than flame,

she wore bracelets and earrings,

round her throat there were golden necklaces,

her delicate bosom shone like the moon.

ABOVE
This image of
Aphrodite is embossed on
a silver medallion,
which was made in
about 300–200BC in
Taranto, Italy.

A handsome young man, Anchises, was seduced by Aphrodite. Terrified when he awoke to find he had slept with a goddess, Anchises believed he would be transformed into an old man on the spot. However, Aphrodite calmed him and promised that the son she would bear from the liaison would resemble a god. The son, Aeneas, became one of the founding fathers of Rome.

Aphrodite protected marriage and cared for young unmarried girls. It was she who was the initial cause of the Trojan War (*see* chapter three). She supported the Trojans in the war, particularly Paris.

POSEIDON

God of the Sea, Poseidon, was also known as the "Earth shaker" because he was the god of earthquakes. He was extremely powerful and there was a belief that he had fought his brother, Zeus, for supreme power. He was certainly a god with power over the other deities if they tried to obstruct him. Poseidon's symbol was a trident, and he is depicted with an enormous and powerful body, which shows him to be a great warrior. Indeed in the battles for supremacy against the Titans and the giants he fought on Zeus's side with great distinction.

Poseidon plotted with Hera and Athena to dethrone his brother, Zeus. He lost that battle and as punishment was sent to the service of Laomedon, King of Troy (and father of Priam), for whom he built the walls of the city. After a year he returned to his home beneath the Aegean Sea "which had been built for him glittering with gold and would last for ever".

Whenever he left his magnificent palace he harnessed horses with golden manes and shod with bronze. Wearing golden armour he hurled his chariot across the waves. If Poseidon was angry, he had the power to make the seas boil and rage in wild tempests. He supported the Greeks in the Trojan War.

APOLLO

Known as "brilliant" or "the fair" or "of the golden locks" Apollo was the god of the light and of harvests. He was the son of Zeus and the goddess Leto, and twin brother of Artemis. Hera's jealousy of Leto was so great she made the birth of the twins one of immense and lengthy suffering. Often illustrated as an archer, Apollo could shoot and kill from very long range. He was also the god of divination, of herdsmen, and, if Homer is to be believed, a musician:

the gods listened to the sound of the glorious lyre which Apollo held.

Apollo was a hard fighter and even dared to challenge the great Hercules to a fight, a stand-off which was only stopped when Zeus stepped in to calm them both down. He was not reluctant to interfere in the affairs of men. When Agamemnon was fighting before the walls of Troy and offended Apollo's priest, the Greek army had to suffer nine days under a hail of Apollo's arrows (*see* chapter five). During the Trojan War Apollo took the side of the Trojans.

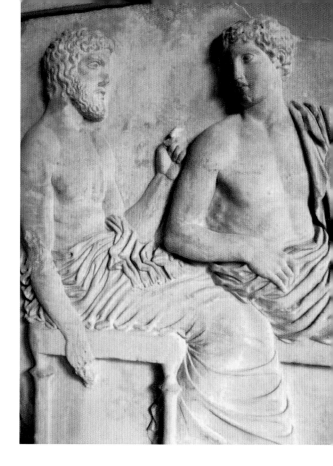

ABOVE *This marble frieze from the Parthenon shows Poseidon and Apollo.*

HERA

Hera was wife, and possibly sister, of Zeus and often known simply as "lady". She was said to be the mother of Ares and of Hebe, the goddess of health. In some versions of the Greek myths, her son, Hephaestus, is believed to be virgin born, as Hera was able to bathe in the spring Kanathos at Nauplia, thus renewing her virginity. While faithful to her serially adulterous husband, Hera was a goddess who could be vindictive and certainly harboured grudges. She was capable driving a girl stark mad for claiming to have more beautiful hair than hers.

Hera could be cruel and fickle. She was extremely jealous of her husband's many infidelities. She did not like Hephaestus as he was crippled, and tried to turn him out of Olympus. She was on bad terms with Aphrodite, whom she envied because Paris had named her "most beautiful" (*see* chapter three), and was not an easy goddess to admire. Her willingness to forgive Zeus despite her jealousy of those he made love to, however, was admirable. This jealousy led to her lending support to the Greeks in the Trojan War.

GODS AND MORTALS

These gods and goddesses have all the characteristics of the men and women who made sacrifice to them. They are capable of love or jealousy, of lust and anger and sometimes of unreasonable prejudices. They may be all-powerful but they are also vulnerable to the actions of their fellows on Olympus. It is of these gods that Homer sings in *The Iliad* and because of these gods that so many men died in the war beneath the walls of Troy.

CHAPTER EIGHT

HECTOR: A TROJAN HERO

The story of the Trojan War has been carried to us by the memories of men for three-a-half thousand years and more. It has changed as each storyteller through the ages has suited the narrative to his style or audience. For example, if the story were told in the palace of a king, the place of Priam or of Agamemnon would be given priority in the narrative. But if the story were told in the home of a warrior, the place of Hector, Achilles or Odysseus would be given more prominence. In this way, these stories have developed over time.

Homer made the epic his own by the sheer genius he brought to the balance of the story. He brought richness to the characters, and was unrelenting in his descriptions of the bravery of men in combat. War itself is never anything but vile and bloody, despite the heroics of some men. It is a story of the darkness of death and of blood seeping into the earth and the sand. It tells of men blinded by death and making the journey from before the wooden gates of the mighty city of Troy along the dark River Styx to the Underworld.

Whatever the causes of the Trojan War, the story is a mighty epic and crosses the thousands of years since its genesis with magnificent ease. And for Homer the war begins with the simple, basic cause… the theft of a wife from her husband.

ON TROY'S HIGH TOWER

Helen, "more lovely than the Moon", was one cause of this great siege, certainly. From time to time she climbed the mighty tower over the south gate of the city and looked

OPPOSITE *A relief of the Trojan War from an amphora found in Mykonos, Greece. It dates from the seventh century BC.*

BELOW *This painting by Gustave Moreau (1826–98) shows Helen standing on the walls of Troy in the place known as Priam's Tower.*

down over the vast army of men camped outside Troy. She looked to the curved prows of the ships in which the army came to Troy when called by Menelaus whom she had betrayed. She could see the tent where cruel, greedy Agamemnon, leader of this vast horde of men who had been besieging the city for ten years, slept.

These Greeks had wives that wept for them and prayed for their return, but Helen did not weep. Beside her stood Priam the King and sometimes Hector, brave brother of Paris. Hector was a mighty hero, and knew how much the women within the city suffered from the siege. He talked and listened to his wife, Andromache, who told how the wives feared the death of their husbands in the plain outside the city walls.

Hector knew his fate was to fight and fight he would. But he did not glory in it. This was unlike the mighty Achilles who sat in the sand by the Greek boats, still brooding after his quarrel with Agamemnon. Hector was as brave as Achilles, but more kindly than his rival. Achilles may have been the greatest hero of the Greeks but he was a fiery, angry, driven and jealous man. When he chose to fight it was wisest to leave the field of battle. However, Achilles still refused to fight.

For ten years the night guards had looked down from the mighty walls of Troy and seen the glittering fires of the besieging army of Greeks. Each morning when it was time to fight the Trojan guards watched the mighty horde marching silently to the walls. For ten years the horde had been there and from time to time the Trojans came from their city and raised their battle cries like the scream of cranes flying noisily south and faced the Greek battle lines.

They skirmished, fought, strewed blood about the land and sent to darkness a thousand men and made widows of their wives, who watched, grieving, from the city walls or waited far away.

AFTER BATTLE

One night, Hector stood in the last light of dusk outside the Trojan walls. Fighting stopped as the sun went down. He turned to his men and called out across the glittering lights of a thousand small cooking fires:

"My comrades, brothers, be men my friends and fight with the courage I know you have. I will go into the city and tell our elders and our wives to prepare sacrifice and to pray to the gods for victory."

THE DEAD

It was normal for any man who killed another in single combat to take the dead man's armour and weapons as his own. It was not unusual for the body of a dead enemy to be treated with disrespect and to be mutilated. For the foot soldier, a common fate was to be left in the battlefield for the scavenging dogs of war and the birds who lived on carrion to feed on the dead who lay about the field after the day of fighting was ended. No army fought after sunset.

It was important for a soldier to feel that his comrades would protect his dead body. They would try to bring a dead comrade back to their lines so that the body could be washed and dressed, and then burned on a funeral pyre. This would ease his soul's way on his journey after death.

In the case of a champion, such as Hector or Achilles, there was an expectation that should they "go into the darkness", their armour and their body would be ransomed to their own side. In this way a wife, a father or his fellow soldiers could ensure that all was done as it should be. It was not unusual for soldiers to gather around a fallen comrade and fight off the enemy intent on stripping the body of its armour.

In cases like that of Patroclus, the dearest friend of Achilles, the richly decorated armour was given to the champion who killed him, in

He turned away then and as he walked, the studded edge of his shield clipped his ankles and his shoulders. The Trojans raised their arms in salute as he went towards the city walls to ask the gods for help for the sake of all of them. When Hector reached the Scaean Gates (the main gates of the city), he was surrounded by wives and daughters of the fighting men out on the plain asking about their husbands, sons and brothers. He did not stop except to ask them all to pray and to tell those whose men had died that they should make sacrifice for their dead.

Hector walked to Priam's magnificent pillared palace. Built of smooth stone there were fifty rooms placed side by side where the sons of Priam and their wives lived. In the courtyard beyond were more bedrooms for the daughters. Hector met his mother there and she asked him to wait while she brought him wine to make a libation to Zeus. Hector refused. He was unclean and could not make sacrifice.

"I am spattered with blood and foul things, mother. Please go to the other women and ask them to make offerings that are clean and unpolluted as I am not. Give to Athena the shawl you most value and vow a sacrifice to her of twelve cattle each year and urge all the women to do the same."

Hector put on his helmet with its long horse-tail crest and went to fetch his brother from Helen's room to take him out to the battlefield. Paris was combing his hair and looking at himself in a mirror, watched sadly by Helen. Disgusted, Hector left without a word.

this case Hector. But Hector was a man who honoured a brave enemy and the body was duly sent back to the Greek lines for the rituals to be performed. It was an act that Achilles, because of his spite and anger, refused to recognize as kindly.

For Achilles the agenda was always personal and never for the greater good. To abuse a fallen hero was a terrible act that not only dishonoured the dead man but dishonoured much more the man who abused his opponent's body. The gods never condoned such acts.

RIGHT *This painting shows Achilles sacrificing Trojan prisoners at the funeral of his friend Patroclus. It dates from the fourth century* BC.

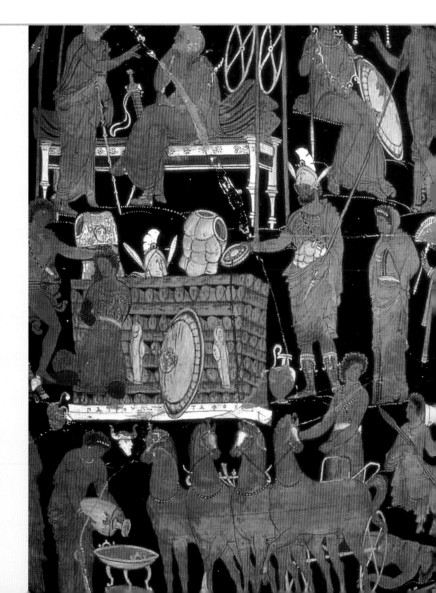

ANDROMACHE

The daughter of Eetion, ruler of the city of Thebes, Andromache was the wife of Hector and mother of his son, Astyanax. She was the epitome of a noble woman. Homer gave her the attributes of courage, dignity and honour. She guarded her husband's reputation, as a wife should.

Her life was marred by tragedy. Achilles slaughtered her father when he captured Thebes, though her mother was spared, ransomed and allowed to go to Troy to live with her daughter. The old lady died before the end of the siege. Andromache was alone when the city fell and she became part of the loot the Greeks took as they pillaged the city. Her baby son, Astyanax, was taken by the looters and thrown from the walls of the city. As Hector foretold on their final meeting, Andromache was handed over to Achilles's son, Neoptolemus, who took her to Greece as a slave.

In Greece, she gave birth to her owner's son, Molossus. When Neoptolemus died she was married off to Helenus – one of the only surviving children of Priam, King of Troy, – who later became ruler of Epirus.

ABOVE *Hector's farewell to his wife Andromache and his son, as depicted by the Venetian painter Luca Ferrari (1606–54).*

On the mighty tower over the Scaean Gates Priam stood with Hector's much-loved wife Andromache and their small son whom he called Scamandrius but whose true name was Astyanax. Fate said he had little time in the world. They waited there and heard below them the sighing of steel as the swords were taken from their leather scabbards.

Hector came to the gate and stopped as he heard Andromache calling his name. Weeping, she came to him, took his hand and spoke quietly to her husband:

"My dear husband please think of your son and even of your wife. This courage of yours will be the end of you. I have no father to comfort me. I have no mother to hold me. My father was killed by Achilles when he sacked my home in Thebes. At least he respected him enough not to despoil his body. Indeed he honoured him. I have no brothers, though once I had seven. All went down to darkness at Achilles's hand. Dear Hector, you are father, mother and brother to me as well as my husband. Do not make your boy an orphan and me a widow."

Hector loved his noble wife but he had to refuse her. He said:

"Andromache, I cannot hide from battle. My fate is decided. I am condemned to it. You think I don't know that Troy is doomed and all its people? You think I don't know that you will be dragged off to Greece slaving for another woman, carrying water, weaving, weeping. Going, when ordered, to another bed.

There goes the wife of Hector, men will say, and you will weep the more. You think I want that? But Fate, my dear wife, decides."

He held out his arms to hold his child and the boy screamed because his father was covered still in blood and filth. Yet he kissed his son, handed him back to his wife and saw that through her tears she was proudly smiling.

"Go home now and do not weep for me. Fate is a thing no man born of a woman can escape. War is men's business and this one is the business of every man in Troy. And of me above all others who call themselves Trojans. For I am Priam's son."

He let her hand go then and walked out of the city to the battlefield. To his joy, he found his brother Paris waiting. Hector was a noble man.

BELOW A vase painting showing Achilles.

ACHILLES SULKS

In the Greek camp, Achilles thought of himself and of the insult he felt had been dealt to him by Agamemnon as the Trojans and the Greeks came to battle again. Standing by his boat, he watched the sand fleas jumping over the mooring rope where it touched the sand. His men were wolf wild to fight, yet he stayed where he was and listened to the distant roar of battle and the high-pitched screaming of the dying as they fell into the darkness. He refused to go into the killing field.

For war was ugly, cruel and unyielding. It was fought hand to hand, shield to shield. It is true that war is only known to men who stand foot to foot, face to face and want nothing but to cut and kill.

CHAPTER NINE

MORTAL COMBAT

The style of warfare described in *The Iliad* was not that of the period in which the Trojan War is set. By Homer's time the tactics and the weapons used in warfare had changed. Homer had only the oral tradition on which he could base his epic descriptions of combat as it was fought by the Greeks and Trojans centuries before.

He describes the battles in vivid detail to emphasize the heroic nature his characters and also provides powerful character sketches of those in the fight. Sometimes the greatest champions, men such as Hector, Ajax or Achilles, delivered a challenge to an enemy champion before a battle began. Then a duel would take place with its own elaborate rules and rituals. There would even be referees to see that no one else interfered. Those duels would temporarily bring the slaughter to a stop as rank-and-file fighting men waited and watched the outcome.

Homer's great skill as a writer allows us, some three millennia later, to taste the full horror of hand-to-hand fighting.

OPPOSITE *A Greek vase painting dating from the late sixth century BC shows fighting at Troy.*

The armies faced each other across the plain. Then they ran at each other with swords and spears at the ready. These bronze armoured men roared into battle and their metal bossed shields crashed into enemy armour. Swords slashed down and thrust hard under the breastbones of the enemy.

Then there came a great moaning from the dying and shouts of joy from the first flush of victors. And the ground ran with blood. The lines of warriors didn't stop. They raced on into the enemy like the roar of waters falling into vast caves.

Antolocus killed the first Trojan. He struck him on the ridge of his thick plumed helmet, on the forehead. The bronze sword point pierced through the bone and darkness covered his arms and he fell as a tower falls. The body was dragged by its feet out of the hot press of the battle.

His armour was stripped off by someone who was not

ABOVE *A Greek warrior in single combat on the Trojan battlefield, carved in the fourth century BC.*

Antolocus, who had killed the dead man. This would bring dishonour to a brave man. The robber was seen and stabbed with a bronze spear in the side where he'd failed to cover himself with his shield. He died.

And over the bodies the Trojans and the Greeks leapt at each other like wolves and men slaughtered men. Eye to eye, foot to foot went on the bloody business of thrusting swords.

Ajax took the life of a young man, Simoisius who was well liked. Ajax struck this young and brave boy as he moved in front of him. He skewered his right breast near the nipple and the bronze spear went through and through his shoulder and he fell like an aspen falls under the axe.

A bright spear thrown to kill Ajax missed its mark but struck Leucus, a true follower of Odysseus, full in the groin. He fell into the darkness across another dead man at his feet.

Odysseus saw what happened to his follower. He cast his glittering spear. It hit Demascoon, the bastard son of Priam, he who loved good horses. The bronze spearhead hit him in the temple and the point came out at the other temple and darkness covered his eyes. He fell with a crash as his armour sounded on the hard ground.

Peirous, son of Imbrassus, threw a jagged stone and stunned Diores and, as he lay on the earth, the thrower ran in on him and stabbed him with his spear beside the navel and his bowels gushed out upon the ground beside him and darkness covered his eyes.

The Iliad, Book IV

The power of the images and the passion with which Homer expresses them has led some people, Heinrich Schliemann among them, to believe that the battles around the walls of Troy are faithfully described. Because Homer's genius brings the characters to life with small details, any reader or listener is convinced this is as it truly was. Although Homer lived at a later time and the methods of war he describes to illustrate the epic are contemporary, he gives a strong sense that this was how it was a thousand years and more before. It was ruthless, opportunistic, bloody and vile.

FORTRESS TROY

A fortified city such as Troy was built within a vast stone wall that acted as the first protection for the most important families. The wall also protected the most reliable source of water and the stores that were preserved in huge jars. Olive oil, grain from the fields outside, dyes, woven cloth, metal objects and the wealth of individual families were all kept behind the huge city walls.

Within their walls the population lived a relatively prosperous life. Because Troy was an important trading post, it had more than its share of materials, gold, dyes and bronze. It attracted the finest of craftsmen who could create beautiful wares from these raw materials. But such wealth was also going to attract raiders. It was against them that the thick walls were built.

The forces that besieged Troy came in open boats from the Aegean and Mediterranean seas. They came considerable distances in their ships, which usually hugged the coast, plundering the hinterland when it suited, destroying and looting cities and villages and taking slaves before moving on. According to Homer, when Priam's son reported back to his father about the numbers of the enemy he had seen disembarking he said: "they are as numerous as the grains of sand on the beach or as the leaves on the trees".

The Iliad describes how the invaders came with chariots that they kept well covered in huts by the shore. Their horses were "of one colour, swift as birds, of the same age and the same height". The use of chariots depended on the enemy emerging from the city gates and deploying into the plain below the walls. If the ground was uneven it made the chariot a questionable means of moving around the field of battle. Homer describes how the chariots racing across the battlefield "threw up so much blood that the axles became caked with the blood of the dead and the dying as they rode over them".

There were also occasions when a good charioteer could deliver an important warrior to the point in the battlefield where he would be most needed. Often the champion, riding behind the charioteer, would throw his lance from this moving platform and then leap down into the melee to confront and insult the particular enemy warrior he was looking for before closing in with his second lance or his bronze sword.

Fighting against and defeating a well-built stone fortress-city took time. In that period the siege towers and covered rams, which were so much a feature in the battles of Alexander the Great in the fourth century BC, did not exist. Breaking through the walls of a great city was not a possibility. Victory relied on starving the people out of the city, hoping the wells within the walls ran dry or destroying their armies when they

ABOVE *Chariots delivered their champions to the areas where the fighting was fiercest.*

came into confrontation in battle. If the raiders could find a traitor within the walls who would open the gates to the enemy then their task would be so much the easier.

Over a third of *The Iliad* is involved in describing either full-blooded battles or single combat. It provides a vivid picture of what such conflicts meant in terms of slaughter, fear, sorrow and the blood of brave men soaking into the land. The battles in *The Iliad* were merciless conflicts that Homer interspersed with savage, one-to-one encounters between the almost godlike heroes of each side. This reliance on heroic champions to demoralize the enemy was a double-edged sword. If, like Achilles, such a hero refused to fight, it was bad for the morale of the fighting soldiers on his side. So Achilles's decision not to go into combat was crucial to the success or failure of the Greeks.

WEAPONS AND ARMOUR

An ordinary foot soldier in Ancient Greece would have worn a leather and metal breastplate and carried a bronze sword and a wooden shafted spear. His shield would have been concave and made from oak planks, which were covered with a thin sheet of bronze. He wore a padded metal helmet, which was very heavy and uncomfortable, to protect his face and the back of his head. It may be that this helmet was only put on as the foot-soldier moved into battle. Foot soldiers wore metal greaves on their legs, which protected their shins, and some also wore a skirt of metal plates to protect the groin, which was a favourite target for spearmen.

In the moment before the lines of soldiers engaged, these men were well disciplined. After that the battle was very much a dark and bloody skirmish with the leaders of the battle only visible in the turmoil while their helmets still carried the brightly coloured tufts of horsehair that decorated them.

Homer gives us a description of the armour Patroclus, best friend of Achilles, borrowed to go into battle when Achilles refused to fight.

Patroclus armed in glittering bronze. First he clipped on his legs beautiful bronze greaves, fastened with silver clasps, and then he drew upon his breast the corselet that once belonged to the swift Aeacides. It flashed like a star with delicate golden inlay.

Over his shoulder he slung his bronze sword inlaid with silver studs. He also carried a long shield and on his noble head he set a finely made helmet with its horse tail crest.

He took up two good spears that fitted his hand. Spears given to his father by Chiron and made to be the death of heroes. Two matched horses were yoked to the chariot, and Pedasus, the greatest horse of all.

The Iliad, Book XVI

And thus Patroclus rode into battle.

BELOW *"The Siege of Troy" by Biagio di Antonio (1476–1504).*

STRATEGY

The tactics of an army besieging a city such as Troy were basic. It was more a war of attrition than of great tactical sweeps and assaults, cunning strategies and the flow of one attack into another. Foot soldiers often fought side by side with their closest friends. Indeed, in Sparta it was policy to place lovers alongside each other (see p.21). In this way commanders ensured that each soldier fought more fiercely in order to protect his partner.

Before the hand-to-hand battle began in earnest, soldiers hurled their metal-tipped spears into the opposing front ranks. If they were provident they might hold on to a spare spear as a long-range weapon for stabbing. It kept them out of the range of enemy swords.

Bowmen were stationed on the flanks of the infantry, letting loose a withering fire until the forces engaged. The bowmen then singled out specific targets and tried to take them out at long range. These archers were often regarded as cowards by the infantry because they kept out of the vicious hand-to-hand fighting.

The killing fields before the walls of Troy ran with blood. Men confronted men eye to eye and hand to hand. Most died at a single swing of the sword or the thrust of a long-handled spear. It was simple: kill or be killed. And the fighting could go on from the rising of the sun to dusk.

Homer tells us that from time to time the fighting stopped so that each army could gather their dead. The slain soldiers were duly honoured, washed, prepared and then burned in funeral pyres. In this respect war was highly ritualized.

In case his men, and particularly his ships, were threatened, Agamemnon had built a fortification: a ridge of sand, stones, earth ramparts and woven wooden hurdles with a ditch in front. Desperate men found the simple defence enough to stop the enemy from rushing onto the beach and firing the ships that lay there. These ramparts were the scene of heroic struggles. Gods were also needed to ensure the safety of the invading fleet from the flaming torches of the Trojans.

The main force of the Trojans could retreat into the huge gates of the city. It was a movement that needed great skill and timing – if it was not planned with great care, such a retreat could end in massive slaughter. Worse, it might let the enemy through the gates into the city. To prevent this, a covered tower in which master archers waited was built on the ramparts. It was built in such a way that the bowmen could fire into the side of the attackers that was unprotected by their shield. This gave covering fire for their own men.

Re-supplying such a vast besieging army cannot have been easy. Some of the warriors would have been deployed in raiding parties, looting cattle, sheep, corn, oil, fruit and whatever else they required. As time went by the Greeks had to raid further and further away from the scene of the siege.

After ten long years many men wanted to go home. Keeping up the morale of the army camped on the beaches was never easy. Games and competitions, weapons practice, running races, wrestling and javelin practice all helped to keep the soldiers occupied.

Ten years is a long time to fight for someone else's wife. This may lend credence to the idea that Helen was never the real cause of the war. Troy was, after all, a city rich in possibilities. As the focus of a number of trade routes, the city was a target for raiders from the south and the east. Men came looking for adventure, slaves, women, gold, bronze weapons and utensils, jewels from the east, rings and necklaces in filigree gold from Scythia and dyes from Persia or the south. These items were a magnet for raiding parties.

BELOW Schliemann unearthed many fine gold beakers and cups, which became part of the treasure lost after the Second World War.

CHAPTER TEN

THE TOWER OF TROY

In April 1872 Schliemann returned to the hillside at Hissarlik. He came on horseback across the plain to the chaos of building blocks and rubble from the mammoth trench that had been dug. He was completely convinced that this hill was the site of Troy. He was certain that the walls he had begun to uncover were those of the Great Tower of Ilium.

From this tower Priam had looked down on the Trojans and the Greeks in battle. Helen had stood beside him and told him the names of the Greek warriors she recognized among the mayhem. From here she saw her abandoned husband Menelaus, the mighty Odysseus, the High King Agamemnon, Patroclus and the great slayer Ajax.

They were not, in fact, the walls Schliemann claimed them to be. Like so much of what he alleged, it was wishful thinking. These exaggerations – and downright lies – gave his critics the ammunition to rubbish his theories.

Bizarrely, Schliemann claimed that Sophia was with him when he returned to the site. He wrote that his wife, whom he described as "an Athenian lady", was a great admirer of Homer. This young woman, he said, knew the whole of *The Iliad* by heart. Schliemann professed that Sophia had been on the dig since the start of the season and was working from morning to night in difficult and dangerous circumstances. It was not true: she was in their house in Athens. He lied, he later said, because he wanted to involve her in his work. He wanted to create a reputation for her as an archaeologist and scholar in her own right. He saw nothing wrong with the lies he told to the learned societies and journals that he continued to bombard with articles and papers.

THE EXCAVATIONS RESUME

The scale of the work Schliemann intended to undertake during this season was vast. He hired a railway engineer, specialist mining equipment, jacks, lifts, crowbars and even battering rams. He employed a Greek foreman who was one of the few men he trusted to ensure that valuable finds were not stolen from the site. It resembled a military operation.

When Sophia did arrive at the dig in May she was given a role as overseer for a section of the wall. The couple lived in a rough house that Schliemann had built on the site. It was convenient and also, no doubt, protected the dig from thieves. It was not easy for Sophia, whose only experience was of city life, to live in such simple conditions. There was also the constant threat of trenches collapsing, malarial mosquitos, noxious fumes from the marshes and deadly vipers. Life was hard for Schliemann's young wife.

The workmen and -women were split into teams to dig separate trenches and deep pits. They also continued to dig the main trench, which was steadily cutting down through the whole hillside. Nothing spectacular was found until Schliemann pushed a wide trench into Frank Calvert's side of the hill.

APOLLO DISCOVERED

In June Schliemann recorded that a relief sculpture of Apollo, the Sun god, had been uncovered. He found a block of marble about six-and-a-half feet (2m) long, nearly three feet high (one metre) and between 14 and 22 inches (35–55cm) thick. A high relief in the middle of the block showed a magnificent carving of Phoebus Apollo dressed in a flowing robe. The figure was chasing across the universe in a chariot pulled by four celestial horses. The horses, which particularly excited Schliemann, were also finely carved, with flaring nostrils and long flowing manes. Above Apollo's long hair and powerfully realized face was a carved disc of the Sun and its rays.

Schliemann made Frank Calvert a pathetically inadequate offer for the piece. Calvert, who had no idea of the commercial value of such work, agreed the price. Schliemann later boasted openly of having "done" the man who had so willingly helped and advised him. He was also obliged by the *firman* to tell the authorities of this find. But he wanted the carved stone for himself and, despite its weight and size, he was determined to spirit it away from the site. In short, he was going to steal it.

Moving the piece was not going to be easy and at one point Schliemann even considered cutting it into three for easy transportation. He justified the idea by claiming that it would improve the piece artistically, and it is true that such things happened regularly in the world of archaeology at the time. Eventually the frieze was smuggled out of the site and shipped to Piraeus. The Turkish authorities had taken Schliemann at his word but they had been hoodwinked. Schliemann never saw anything wrong in what he had done, but then he could not see anything wrong in anything he decided to do.

The frieze was taken from Piraeus to Schliemann's garden in Athens. It was a reminder to the Turkish authorities that they could not trust Schliemann or, indeed, other archaeologists to honour any agreements they signed. On Schliemann's death the Apollo frieze was sent to the Berlin Ethnological Museum.

THE DIG CONTINUES

BELOW *A deep trench dug directly through the hillside at Hissarlik, from an engraving made in 1873.*

The digging went ever deeper. Schliemann had a huge platform constructed through the hill. It was built 46 feet (14m) into the earth and extended round all his previous trenches. His engineers estimated that he had already removed over 100,000 cubic yards of material. There were difficulties and dangers in the dig. The walls of various trenches had collapsed, and, on one occasion, a number of workers were buried. Schliemann, who conceded that the work was risky, was concerned that they might not come out alive. However, they all survived and the digging went on as it had before. There was a mutiny among the workers when he stopped them taking breaks to smoke – he would not allow the dig to slow down.

Conditions were uncomfortable. Malarial mosquitoes caused outbreaks of fever at the site and potentially lethal bites from the masses of dangerous vipers in the area were a matter for concern. Local people had an antidote that they claimed was effective against the venom and it seemed to work. Ever the businessman, Schliemann even considered having the antidote analysed and patented. He never quite stopped being a hustling salesman.

The removal of debris from each layer revealed by the trench went on faster and faster. In seventeen days at the start of the season, the workers removed over 600 cubic yards (549 cubic metres) of material every day. There is no doubt that this material would have contained finds that would have been invaluable to a scholar archaeologist. But Schliemann's only concern was the fame that he assumed would be his when he discovered Homer's Troy and the wealth that he was certain lay there.

DISCOVERIES

Pots, Stone-Age ware, votive figures, owl-headed vessels, spinning whorls and small amounts of iron ware were regularly found but little was discovered to indicate that the flourishing Hellenic civilization of Schliemann's dreams had inhabited the site.

At the beginning of August, when the summer heat must have been intolerable, he was still actively involved in the digging. On the south side of the hill near his transverse trench Schliemann discovered a tower. It was about forty feet thick and blocked the trench. He decided to dig around it, as he was certain that at last the hill was revealing its secrets.

He was convinced that the view from this tower would have taken in the Plain of Troy, the Aegean Sea and the islands of Tenedos, Imbros and Samothrace. In short, Schliemann assumed that this was the great Tower of Troy, the same tower that Andromache climbed when she heard that the "Trojans were hard pressed and the power of the enemy was great". It was a supreme moment for Schliemann. The tower had been buried for thousands of years and when he finally uncovered it in all its magnificence, he believed it would stand as a great monument to Greek heroism – and, of course, to himself.

ABOVE *Cleaning ancient pottery with more painstaking methods than Schliemann used.*

Schliemann claimed that the tower would forever be a beacon that would be seen by anyone who sailed through the Hellespont. He hoped that it would become a place to which the best and most intelligent young people from Europe would come as pilgrims. He wrote that he wanted no reward for his huge expense and suffering except that the "civilized world" would give him the right to rename the hill and call it Troy.

Whatever right he looked for from the "civilized world", it hardly mattered. Yet again he had jumped to conclusions without foundation. This was not the great tower of Troy and the season's dig was over.

On his next visit to the site he would find gold. And again he would jump to the wrong conclusions. The gods had the habit of mocking the vanity of mortals and they did not give up the habit even in 1872.

CHAPTER ELEVEN

PARIS MEETS MENELAUS

When their favourites were under threat in combat, the gods took sides. If it were necessary, they would find a way to rescue their favoured mortal from danger. Often they would hide them in clouds or whisk them from the battlefield. Homer could well have used this device as a euphemism for the cowardice of some of the mortals who were protected in this manner, among them Paris.

THE SHAME OF PARIS

Paris had been shamed when his brother Hector, still reeking of blood from the battlefield, found him in Helen's room combing his hair. Hector was disgusted at his brother's vanity and his cowardice. The beautiful Paris knew he had to make some sort of impression or the Trojan soldiers would do more than whisper that all this fighting and slaughter was on account of the long-haired, smiling Helen. They might even decide to hand her back to her husband.

Paris knew that Menelaus was older than he was and that he had been fighting for a very long time. He must be feeling weary from the pace of battle by now. Paris realized that he had to take a gamble. He knew he could count on Aphrodite if he needed help and he was going to need her. So Paris decided to challenge Menelaus, husband of Helen, to mortal combat. The winner would take Helen as a prize and the result would end the war.

THE FIGHT FOR HELEN

Paris walked into the no-man's land outside the gates of Troy. He was magnificently dressed: a leopard skin lay across his shoulders, a bow and a quiver full of arrows hung from one shoulder, he carried his silver-studded sword, two bronze-headed spears and a bronze-bossed shield. Standing in the morning light he looked across the army of the Greeks and challenged any man to fight him. He knew Menelaus would not resist the challenge. The Trojans roared their approval.

Menelaus, a favourite of the god Ares, saw who was making the challenge and was as glad as a lion coming on the carcass of a wild goat. He leapt from his chariot to the dusty ground and strutted through his army to confront the man who had stolen his wife. Menelaus was tall; he may have been older than Paris, but he was a great warrior

and he was fearless. His weapons were battered with the signs of war: dented, stained with blood, chipped and hacked by the weapons of his enemies. He stood and looked at his rival with contempt.

Paris looked into the eyes of Menelaus and saw death. Shamefully he retreated into the Trojan lines where he was concealed. The Greeks roared, mocking him as a coward. Hector, his brother cursed him and called out:

"Paris, you are nothing but a pretty thing. All you're good for is to seduce women. It would be better if you had died than be shown to be such a coward. You dishonour your father our king. You were brave enough to steal another man's wife when his

back was turned. And yet dare not test yourself against her husband when he offers fair combat to settle the matter. Music won't protect you nor your long hair, nor all the gifts of Aphrodite. If we Trojans had been braver you would long ago have been dead for the evils you have made us suffer."

The Trojan warriors muttered then in anger and Paris knew they were turning against him. Ashamed, he stood and walked back through the Trojan ranks. He agreed to fight the mighty Menelaus and made an offer:

"Whoever wins may take Helen and all she owns and after it is done let our Trojans live in fertile Troy and the Greeks go home to Argos of the horse-meadows and the place of beautiful women."

The fickle Trojan army roared its agreement. The Greeks roared too for they saw a way to settle the matter and return to their families. They had every faith in Menelaus defeating this pretty young man. Hector stood between the lines so that the Trojans could not advance beyond his spear. He called on Agamemnon to accept his brother's offer. But it was Menelaus who spoke.

"This trouble touches me most and I know both armies want an end to it. So, whichever of us is fated to die, let him die and the rest of you can go to your homes."

Then the Greeks cheered their brave hero and the wronged husband of Helen again. The armies sat in lines, laid their swords and shields on the ground and stuck their spears into the earth beside them. They were not a spear's throw from each other. Aphrodite looked down from Olympus and saw her favourite preparing for the fight to come. She was worried. Zeus ordered her not to interfere, for she would risk his anger.

Priam came from the city with two lambs and Agamemnon brought lambs from the boats on the sand where Achilles still sulked. Helen watched from the tower over the Scaean Gate. Priam cut the throats of the lambs and let them bleed as sacrifice to the gods. Agamemnon did the same. The Trojan king, who could not bear to watch his son fight the mighty Menelaus, rode back into his city through the Scaean Gates. He climbed the tower to stand beside the lovely Helen.

Hector and Odysseus met between the lines of men. The mighty champions nodded gravely at each other with respect. They stood back to back and paced out the killing ground. Then they called the two men to the mark. Lots were cast from Hector's helmet to see who would have first cast of his javelin. Hector cast the die; Paris won the right to make the first throw.

On the tower Helen looked across the lines of men and saw her husband Menelaus. She recalled her life with him and her daughter, Hermione, whom she had left behind and tears came to her eyes. She pointed out the leaders of the Greek army to Priam and Andromache, Hector's wife. Agamemnon, brother of Menelaus, was there of course and standing proud as a ram among the ranks of men was the wily Odysseus,

ABOVE A blue faïence figure of Aphrodite, who favoured Paris on the battlefield.

shorter by a head than Agamemnon, but broader of breast and shoulder; the mighty fighter Ajax could be seen and near him, among his dark Cretans, was Idomeneus. Helen searched for her brothers, Castor and Polydeuces, but she looked in vain, for they had already gone into the darkness.

Between the ranks of seated warriors below, the two champions stood in their allotted killing ground. Hector looked across at Odysseus and each stepped to one side and held a spear across his thighs. No man was allowed to come past those spears and interfere in the duel that was about to begin.

All was ready. The excited chatter of the seated soldiers stopped. A soft breeze moved the horsehair crest on Hector's helmet. Then Paris raised his arm. He leaned back a little and threw his spear straight at the mighty Menelaus, favourite of Ares. The spear struck his shield.

Then it was the turn of Menelaus. He hurled his javelin towards the shield of Paris. It tore through the shield and the breastplate. The bronze head touched the skin of the Trojan but drew no blood. Agitated, Aphrodite watched. She had already moved to deflect the spear. Zeus growled at her not to interfere.

The rivals faced each other, grasping their bronze swords. The troops sat silent watching and eager. Beyond them carrion birds waited: their time would come. Menelaus prayed to mighty Zeus: "Let him be humbled by me and then men will fear forever to injure and dishonour their host."

He moved in closer. Big as he was, Menelaus was fast on his feet. He avoided Paris's weapon and, rising high on his feet, he swung his silver sword at his rival's head, shattering it on the rim of his helmet. Aphrodite made ready to move from Olympus and protect her champion. Ares nudged the mighty Zeus and Aphrodite restrained herself.

APHRODITE INTERVENES

Before Paris could react, Menelaus threw aside the broken sword, stepped even closer, and took Paris's helmet in his hands, twisting it and attempting to choke his enemy with the ox hide strap that held it in place. Aphrodite saw her favourite close to death. Before Zeus could stop her, the anxious goddess saved Paris by cutting the strap. Menelaus was left on the battlefield, holding the empty helmet. Paris had disappeared. Aphrodite had hidden the handsome young man in a mist and spirited him to Helen's bedroom.

Menelaus looked about, searching the Trojan lines for signs of the beautiful youth. He demanded that Paris be brought back to the mark. If the Trojan warriors could have found him there is no doubt they would have thrown him back into the killing field. Paris and his cowardice had dishonoured them again.

Helen left the tower and walked through the stone streets to her home. She found Paris in her bedroom. At first she was ashamed of him, her true husband had seemed such a powerful magnificent warrior that for a moment she had regrets. Still filthy

 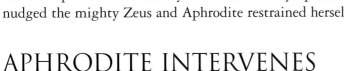

with sweat and the dust of the battlefield, Paris demanded that she come to bed. At first Helen protested, but she could not resist the will of Aphrodite.

Meanwhile Zeus, angry at Aphrodite's interference, sat in council with wide-eyed Hera and Athena. The goddesses wanted battle to resume. The men below were still sitting facing each other in truce. Zeus angrily agreed that the war should begin again. Disguised as an old and famous warrior, Athena visited the Trojan lines where she sought out Lucaon's son, a decent young man and an archer. She urged the boy to kill Menelaus with a well-fired arrow. The young man shot at the warrior from behind the Trojan lines but Zeus saved the Spartan king from death by deflecting the arrow that would have killed him. The truce was broken and the terrible business of war continued.

WOMEN IN THE ANCIENT WORLD

The lives of the goddesses reflected the position of women in the society of Ancient Greece. They attempted to assert themselves but, by and large, Zeus held the reins and even immortal women usually had to do as they were ordered.

Women in Homer's time were not noticeable in public life except in the most singular of circumstances. They lived in quarters that were designated "the women's rooms". It was possible to lock and bar these rooms and so to hide women from the outside world. Men never allowed their wives to entertain guests. Women who did appear at meals were courtesans called *heterae*. These women were trained in the art of conversation, respected for their education and wit but at the same time, they were not quite respectable, sometimes providing sexual favours. Female slaves who were captured on raids or bought in markets existed for the sole purpose of taking care of the house.

The place for a wife or a daughter was inside the house and this was where they remained except to attend religious festivals that were specifically female. It was difficult for a married woman to escape from the home. Slaves did the heavy work and men went to the market to purchase the necessary provisions. The province of a rich man's wife was to have legitimate heirs and to manage domestic affairs. In many ways, this was similar to the position of women in the Victorian era.

While the Greeks of Homer's time were keen for their sons to be educated in the art of public speaking, logic, music, the sciences and literature, there was no way that a girl might get that sort of education if she came from a "good" family. Women of "respectable" families were expected to accept their place. They could neither vote nor own property. Their husbands dealt with any legal matters that concerned them. Daughters were given away in arranged marriages and were then owned by their spouse until one or the other died. Even a widow was automatically

WHISPERS BEGIN

The citizens of Troy were more and more unsettled by the seige. Their young men were dying on the Scamander plain or dragging themselves, wounded, into the shelter of the walls. They watched Helen, the cause of all their sorrows, walking through their streets; they had not allowed her to stay in Troy because they wanted her there. The ordinary men and women would have let Helen go. But she was under the protection of Priam who excused her any blame for the war, believing the gods had started the conflict. And if that was the king's opinion, there could be no argument. Women, after all, were owned through marriage or conquest. It was like that then.

placed under the guardianship of her nearest living male relative. The lives of women in Ancient Greece appear to have been bounded by the hearth, the loom, the domestic round and bringing up children.

With no possessions or freedom of her own, and a servant to her husband, the life of a married woman seems to have been an unhappy one. What place could love, companionship and even honour have in their lives? And yet in the relationship between Hector and Andromache or Odysseus and Penelope, Homer provides evidence of a different aspect to the relationships between men and women. Both these couples show deep loyalty and friendship towards their spouses. Homer writes that there is nothing more powerful than when a man and his wife live together in true unity, sharing the same ideas and thoughts. Here lies the secret to the best position a wife could make for herself. If she were intelligent enough, her husband would look to her for advice and companionship. Tradition might demand that she was subservient, but a wife was very often more influential than it might seem.

The example of the gods also gave women the licence to be rather freer than might appear to be the case. Zeus might make rules, but Hera used her feminine wiles to outwit him. Aphrodite may be ordered to do one thing and actually do another, but her defiance did not often get punished and she would even turn the punishment to her own advantage. Athena might be told to leave the battlefield alone but she was cunning enough to choose the right moment to persuade Zeus that her way would be best.

BELOW *A terracotta figure of a woman performing domestic chores.*

CHAPTER TWELVE

GOLD

◆◆◆

Heinrich and Sophia Schliemann returned to Hissarlik in January 1873. Between visits, he had travelled to various academic institutions and academies, but he had either been ignored or criticized by many of Europe's archaeological experts and historians. Only in Britain, where knowledge of The Iliad and of Virgil's Aeneid was regarded as the mark of a civilized man, did he find encouragement. Prime Minister Gladstone was certainly a keen advocate of Schliemann's achievements.

TRIUMPH OVER ADVERSITY

Above all, Schliemann wanted to be recognized as the highest authority on Troy by the university professors he admired in Germany, home of his harshest critics. These professors refused to accept that Schliemann might have solved the ancient mystery of the whereabouts of Troy. They resented this interloping businessman – he had no academic background so how dare he presume to tell them that he had discovered Homer's Troy? There were also still many who regarded the whole matter as ridiculous, believing that Troy was merely a figment of an ancient poet's imagination.

Letters flew back and forth, with professors debunking him and newspaper editors mocking him. Schliemann knew that the next dig had to provide his detractors with more than stones and pottery artefacts, with more than bronze bowls and votive figures. It was time to uncover something spectacular.

This season would mean make or break. As usual Schliemann was determined to keep anything he found of value. He may have agreed to the Turkish government's demand that any finds were split fifty-fifty but he had no intention of keeping to that agreement.

It is worth noting that the Greeks had a very serious policy of trying to retain any archaeological discoveries within Greece. Their experience with Lord Elgin, the English ambassador to Athens who had taken several marble sculptures from the Parthenon, rankled, as it still does today. In other countries around the Middle East archaeologists had to agree with the authorities to leave finds in situ or to pass them on to the best local museum.

It was not, as Schliemann was to declare, unknown for authorities to demand that any finds were to remain in the country of origin. Schliemann had already broken his agreements with the Turks by stealing the Apollo frieze and installing it in his garden in Athens. To counter any repetition of such plunder the Turks had placed an overseer on the site to ensure that this did not happen again. It was perhaps a case of too little and too late, for Schliemann was a cunning man.

The Schliemanns arrived at the site too early in the year to begin the dig. Both Heinrich and Sophia suffered from the cold wind that blew across the plain. Impatient to proceed, Schliemann soon had a team of men cutting a trench in a northwesterly direction "from the south eastern corner of the Acropolis". He was determined that this expedition would reveal the accuracy of his prediction that this was Priam's city.

Schliemann never concentrated his efforts on exploratory trenches or small excavations. Everything had to progress at speed. By the beginning of March he had uncovered what he called a temple to Athena. Ten feet (three metres) below the floor of the temple he discovered a huge number of vast earthen jars (*pithoi*), some of which were over six feet (two metres) tall. They had served to store oil, grain or water at times of trouble.

The site of the temple stood in the way of Schliemann's continued excavation of what he claimed was the Tower of Troy. He decided to leave only a few stones of the temple standing. It was sacrificed in his urgent scramble to reveal the entire tower. The tower confirmed his belief that the buildings were part of Troy and that the siege was the reason for such huge *pithoi*.

Spring was beginning to break out and flowers covered the marshy plains. There were the usual troubles with illness and Schliemann dosed the local villagers with

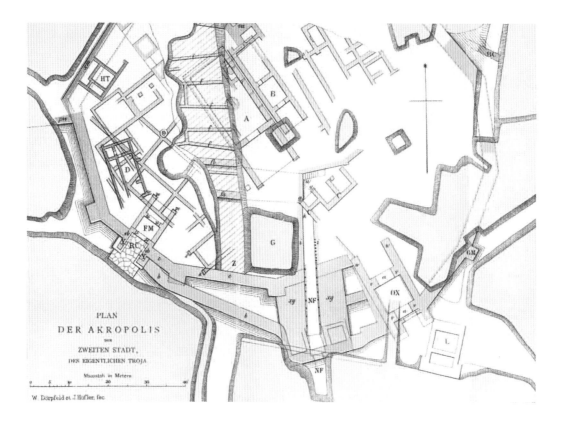

quinine in an attempt to keep malaria at bay. The dig continued to be physically dangerous as the trenches scattered haphazardly about the site went deeper and deeper. His workers demanded more money to toil in such conditions.

Schliemann had trouble with some workers who had been stealing gold objects from the site. One man had been caught when his wife foolishly wore stolen ornate gold earrings and necklace in public only to be reported to the police by a jealous neighbour. Schliemann was not going to take a chance of that happening again so he instigated a system of rewards for anything brought to him by the diggers.

By now Schliemann was receiving visitors to the site. Everyone from mistrustful academics to German aristocrats wanted to see what he was doing. The academics complained that the methods Schliemann used were still not protecting the artefacts on the site. One archaeological layer was mixed with another as he hurried down into the hillside. But Schliemann ignored any suggestion that he should take a more scientific way. As ever, he knew best.

Schliemann and his men removed vast quantities of earth from the site and revealed more stone walls. The main walls ran through the site on both sides of a trench dug through the whole hill at a depth of 39 feet (13m). Schliemann wrote about finding a building in which slabs of stone were laid in such a way that they must have been part of a religious structure. The slabs lay about three feet below a sacrificial altar and formed a channel of green slate, which he believed was there to carry away blood. There was evidence of a huge fire destroying the city at the level at which the remains of the altar were found. He left the altar where it was so that visitors to the site could see that he had not exaggerated or lied about his finds.

As his workers dug into the hill thousands more finds were made. Pottery shards, metal pins and nails, lance heads, pots, pithoi and pottery spindles for spinning wool lay about the site or were taken into the wooden hut in which the Schliemanns now lived. They were not methodically recorded when taken out of the earth as they were not what he wanted. A terracotta hippopotamus that was found at a level of 23 feet (seven metres) surprised Schliemann. He believed that the hippopotamus occurred only in rivers in the interior of Africa. He then noted that Herodotus wrote about these animals being worshipped in Egypt. So this red terracotta figurine had come from the Upper Nile. This certainly added credence to the belief that Troy was a key trading post on routes that extended as far as Egypt.

As the weather improved, Schliemann's dig revealed a long stretch of paved road. Buildings had lined the road but they had been burned at some point. The rooms were filled with black, red and yellow wood ash that may have been the remains of decorated wooden pillars that divided the rooms. He decided that the flagged road led to the Scaean Gate of the city. He then proceeded to uncover a gate complete with its own tower. An excited Schliemann read Homer again and believed that from this tower Priam and Helen could have looked across the plain to the two armies facing each other.

He decided that in order to dig out more huge quantities of material from the ever-widening trench he should square off the walls. This would also make them slightly safer from the falls that plagued the work from time to time. In May he declared that the wall he was digging along was definitely the side of Priam's palace.

Schliemann was certain that Priam and Paris walked these wide pavements and that Helen and Andromache had lived among the buildings he was revealing. Proof was not something he much cared about. All he had to do was make a spectacular find and people would then begin to listen to him and to respect him. Schliemann was about to discover what he regarded as the spectacular evidence he needed to show that the events of *The Iliad* were historical fact.

ABOVE *A collection of Trojan vases and other terracotta vessels found by Schliemann during the dig in 1873.*

RIGHT *The paved ramp that led down to the Scaean Gate in the walls of the city.*

SCHLIEMANN'S TALE

On June 17, 1873 he wrote about his discovery, claiming it was his own sharp sight that led to the find that would make him famous.

On this day in June, the overseer for the Turkish government was at the site, as was Schliemann's trusted Greek foreman, Nikolaos Zathyros. A large workforce was cutting into the various trenches. In one trench, one wall of which he claimed was part of Priam's palace, Schliemann spotted a curved copper article in the wall, which he later claimed was a shield (it is more likely that it was a basin). Behind this object, he alleged that he glimpsed gold.

Schliemann quickly called a meal break. The Turkish workers were glad to drop their tools and get into the shade to rest and to eat. He told his foreman that as it was his birthday all the men could have an extra hour off. He claimed later that he did this to stop the greedy workers from stealing the items he had seen in the trench wall. This is somewhat ironic when one considers what he did subsequently.

Schliemann claimed that he quietly called Sophia to come and look at what he had seen. They slipped away into the deep trench. Together they walked back to the section of wall where he believed he had caught a glimpse of gold. He began to cut

into the wall. This was not without risk as there was always considerable danger that the pile might fall and crush him – or that he would be seen. But Schliemann was determined to get the treasures out. Sophia stood by ready to pack the treasures into her shawl and to carry them away. It was a considerable find.

The treasure, Schliemann declared, had probably been packed into a wooden box in haste, perhaps as the city was being pillaged. In the same part of the trench he found a large silver jar, in the bottom of which were two magnificent gold filigree diadems; a breast plate; nearly nine thousand exquisitely worked small gold rings; gold bracelets; two small gold goblets and 56 gold earrings of filigree work.

It was a magnificent find. Even though he had agreed that the authorities were to share half of the find with him, he would still have had a considerable and valuable treasure. However, Schliemann decided to conceal the lot from the Turks.

Schliemann brought the treasures to the couple's wooden house. The Turkish official, suspicious, came and demanded to know what had been going on. Schliemann, in no uncertain terms, told him to clear off. The official left the site to tell his superiors, a day's ride away, that something suspicious was occurring. While he was away Schliemann asked Frank Calvert if he would take delivery of some bags in which the finds were hidden. Calvert agreed and that night they were taken to his

THE TREASURE OF KING PRIAM OF TROY

The items that Schliemann discovered at Hissarlik in June 1873 included:

1. A large copper shield, which may actually have been a copper bowl.
2. A copper cauldron, which Schliemann claimed was Homeric.
3. A copper plate, which Schliemann claimed was bent as a result of great heat.
4. A small copper vase.
5. A small round gold bottle weighing around 1lb troy weight (the measurement used for gems and precious metals).
6. A gold cup weighing 7oz troy weight.
7. A gold cup or drinking vessel with two spouts.
8. A small Electro (gold and silver mix) cup.
9. Six silver knife blades that had been hammered into shape.
10. Thirteen copper lances.
11. A large copper key (Schliemann claimed that it fitted the wooden box in which the treasure must have been stored).

house. The Turkish official returned to the site and Schliemann sent him away rudely refusing to allow him or anyone else to see what he and his wife had brought out of the trench.

By this time the gold and jewels had vanished. They would eventually turned up on display in Schliemann's house in Athens. He knew he had not honoured the agreement he had signed to obtain permission to dig but he could not resist the temptation to boast and to crow about what he had done. Schliemann claimed that the agreement was broken when the Turks refused him permission to take anything he had found out of Turkey. He used this as a flimsy excuse for smuggling the treasure into Greece.

When he showed off the vast number of objects that he had found, which included not only the gold but amphorae, terracotta bowls, figurines, axe heads, blades and iron rings, he believed that the international academic community would acclaim him as an equal. He also appeared to believe that the Greek government would welcome the treasures of their ancient ancestor sbeing returned to Greek hands. Schliemann justified his theft by stating that there was no museum suitable to house finds in Turkey.

He was to be disappointed with the reaction he received. An angry Frank Calvert, whom Schliemann had already cheated out of a decent price for objects he had removed from his area of the land, accused him of being

LEFT A *highly decorated pin with quadrangular head. It was found by Schliemann at the site.*

OPPOSITE *Priam's Treasure displayed, the bounty included gold beads, necklaces, bronze bowls, axe heads, gold cups and terracotta vessels.*

neither a gentleman nor a man of honour. Perhaps Calvert knew what trouble this wholesale theft and boasting would bring. Schliemann had, he said, defrauded Turkey in the name of science. Calvert and the other archaeologists feared that by his actions Schliemann had ensured that no one would trust the word of any archaeologist.

However, Schliemann was not interested in what men like Calvert thought. He now regarded himself as the most important archaeologist in the world. He continued to brag of what he had done at talks and meetings around the world. In newspapers and journals he lectured the experts and dismissed their opinions as jealous hot air. Schliemann was known to have told a number of boastful lies. And now came the serious questions.

Why had Schliemann lied about his wife being at the dig all the time? He claimed to have found the ashes of Odysseus and his wife Penelope, but where was the proof? His trusted foreman, Nikolaos Zathyros, contradicted Schliemann's story, claiming that it was he who helped carry the treasure from where it was found and not Sophia. Then, more damagingly, the foreman said that he didn't remember much in the way of gold items. If this was the case then why believe anything Schliemann said about his find? The Greek foreman also said that the key, which Schliemann alleged came from the chest in which the treasures must have been buried, was found in another part of the site altogether. Schliemann might bluster or deny but the questions went on being asked.

Maybe Schliemann had lied about other matters too. One thing was certain: he desperately wanted to discover a major find at the site. The treasure had been smuggled out of the site without any proper details being taken of the exact level at which each item was found. Rumours suggested that perhaps the treasure was forged or maybe Schliemann had put together various smaller finds to create one vast find. Had he taken objects from other sites? Schliemann was certainly a liar, but was he a forger too?

The arguments about the find have never ceased. Whatever its provenance, treasure was there to see. Eventually it was shown at the British Museum in London, where it was a sensation. Schliemann and Sophia were lionized by society in the English

ABOVE *Sophia Schliemann wearing golden necklaces, a headpiece and earrings from Priam's treasure.*

RIGHT *Detail of gold earring from the treasure, which dates from about 2300BC.*

capital. He lectured at the Society of Antiquarians in London and was entertained by the Prime Minister.

After numerous lawsuits he was eventually allowed to keep the treasure by paying a very small part of its value to the Turkish government. But what was to happen to the treasure? Schliemann appears to have bought the recognition he craved by offering it to the Prussian government. It came at a cost. Schliemann was determined that those who had ridiculed him for so long would pay a heavy price for the gift.

In 1881 he and Sophia went to Berlin. There, in a lavish ceremony, where he was guest of honour, the treasure was formally handed over to the state. It would be housed in a new section of Berlin Museum called the Schliemann Museum. He insisted that he be made a freeman of the city and that he was awarded a Prussian order with a medal for his wife. He was also to be made a member of the Prussian Academy of Sciences.

The magnificent Trojan treasure included not only the gold but urns and coins, copper battleaxes, owl-faced pots and figurines, terracotta basins, bowls, jars and vases. All this paid for Schliemann's vain determination to be praised and recognized by the academics. He had got what he wanted by sticking to his doubtful tactics. Rather as Achilles achieved what he wanted eventually. But the price Achilles paid was terrible.

BELOW In 1881, Priam's treasure was housed in Berlin in a museum building named after Schliemann. After the Second World War ended in 1945, it lay amongst these ruins.

CHAPTER THIRTEEN

A BLOODY BATTLE

◆◆

The siege of Troy went on and still Achilles sulked by his boat. Gulls hopped and pecked at the weeds that lifted and fell with the slight movement of the water. The Greeks might desperately need him in battle but he was not moving.

SPIES

The old fox Odysseus and the mighty warrior Diomedes tried to persuade Achilles to join the fight. He refused them, as he had refused the gifts sent to him by Agamemnon. Odysseus tried again but Achilles reminded him that Agamemnon had taken Briseis, the girl who was given to him as his rightful property for bravery in battle. No man – not even Agamemnon – could steal her. It was dishonourable. He would not fight and he would not forgive his king.

Achilles went on to tell Odysseus that Agamemnon was jealous of his courage. Worse, for a man in such a position to be greedy with those he commands makes him an unworthy king.

"I would not have any daughter of his as my wife even if he offered someone as lovely as Aphrodite or as wise as Athena. I will not fight for him."

With that he wrapped himself in his bearskin cloak and turned his back on Odysseus, who walked away across the camp and past the sleeping men. Odysseus and Diomedes were shocked by the anger between these two great men. Diomedes felt insulted by Achilles, there would be a bloody battle the next day and he knew the Greeks were not as well prepared as they should be. They needed Achilles.

Odysseus reported to Agamemnon. He told him exactly what Achilles had said. The other chiefs were there and were angry too. Diomedes turned on Odysseus and accused him of being too easy on the sulking Achilles.

"You go to a man like that and beg him to join us. It is unworthy of you, my friend. You only feed his pride. We're on our own and must prepare for the fight without him."

Agamemnon said nothing except to boast that they would defeat the Trojans without their hero. No one said anything to that. No one believed it, least of all Agamemnon. Odysseus put an arm around Diomedes and he and his old friend walked out into the moonlight. Warriors slept on the sand, their spears stuck upright and close to hand. Nestor, a wise and older chief, joined them.

"We need to know who is in the field against us, and where they plan to attack. If we have to fight them without Achilles we need all the help we can find."

The warrior chiefs agreed that they needed to know as much as they could but it would need a brave man to cross into the enemy lines and find someone who would tell them what they needed to know. Diomedes offered to go across the plain and into the enemy camp if Odysseus would come with him. He knew that Odysseus had never been able to resist the idea of an adventure. Quickly they prepared, as they had to go while the Moon was waning and the Sun was not yet creeping over the land.

Diomedes took up a two-edged sword and a shield. Odysseus took a bow, a quiver full of arrows and his bronze sword. His helmet was leather with a soft cap under it and his shield was edged with white boar's teeth. They were ready. The two men slipped quietly away from the Greek camp and crossed through the narrow gap in the earthworks that surrounded the boats. They warned the sentry not to raise the alarm when they returned and that they would signal, making a call like a bittern when they approached.

In the dark a heron clattered into the air from the marshy land. Odysseus took it as a signal from Athena so the pair stopped and prayed to the goddess for success in their mission. Then they slipped across the shadowed ground towards their enemy. As they moved slowly and silently towards the Trojan forces they saw a figure flitting towards them from the enemy lines. They lay silent in the shadows of a rock and let him pass. The solitary figure was wearing a wolf skin cloak and carried a short spear and a sword: he was a Trojan spy.

Odysseus and Diomedes followed the figure. As the Moon appeared from behind a ragged cloud, the Trojan saw them and began to run, but it was hopeless. Diomedes let fly his spear and almost hit his enemy. The Trojan tripped, lost his sword and tried to run on. The two Greek warriors closed on him. Two against one: the Trojan had no chance and, weeping with fear, surrendered to them.

"Please," he begged them, "please don't kill me. I am Dolon and my father is a rich man. He will pay well for me alive. Please…"

Odysseus smiled at the terrified Trojan and demanded to know who had sent him. It had been Hector, with the promise that Dolon would receive the chariot and horses of Achilles if he spotted a weakness in the Greek lines. Diomedes smiled too and asked the frightened man about the passwords that would get them past the Trojan guards. Dolon, the coward, told them what they wanted to know.

Odysseus asked more and Dolan, kneeling, spewed up the answers, believing he'd saved his skin. Behind him Diomedes stood with his sword in hand. Dolon begged to be set free, but Diomedes slashed hard and fast at the bent neck of the sorry man. The Trojan was dead before he stopped pleading.

They left him where he fell, moved into the lines of sleeping Trojans, gave passwords and moved on. They came as they intended to the guards sleeping around the magnificent white horses and ivory and gold chariot of the King of Thrace. Silently they butchered the guards and harnessed the horses. Diomedes and the wild warrior Odysseus leapt into the chariot and raced laughing through the enemy lines and back to their camp. In the morning the two men gave an offering to mighty Athena. They told all they had learned from Dolon, who had revealed the Trojan passwords, the position Hector would take in the battle and Trojan plans to fire the Greek ships.

The Greek army woke under the dawn light, lit fires, warmed themselves, stretched, checked their swords and spears and their bronze-covered shields. They understood how desperate their situation was without Achilles. They had been forced back almost to the barricade they had built of sand and rocks. It was all that protected their ships from the enemy. The sun flew higher into the sky. Both armies were prepared for another day of battle.

On Mount Olympus Zeus again warned the gods, on pain of being cast out, to take no part in the coming battle. Fate would decide the future of Helen of Troy and the warriors on the plain. The gods and goddesses lowered their heads in submission, all that is except Hera, Zeus's wife. For Hera had a plan to aid the Greek warriors in this time of terrible danger and Poseidon was prepared to help if Zeus could be distracted.

BELOW *The Greek warrior Achilles in his armour.*

BATTLE

Hector strode about the plain among the Trojans and their allies. He came upon Paris and reminded him that today he was not to abandon his men for Helen's bed. Paris was angry at his brother's words. Hector looked about the men in Paris's command and saw there were some men missing. Where were Asius, Helenus, Othryoneus and their men? The walls of Troy would come crashing down without the help of any Greek warriors, if such allies were lost. Paris admitted they had gone but he swore he had strength enough to make up for these missing men and promised he would fight with the best of warriors.

Hector turned away then. He walked back to the lines of his mighty army. They stood poised to roar down on to the barricades of wood and sand that stood between them and the long curved black-hulled ships where Achilles still sat. They would burn the Greek ships before the Sun set. Hector stood between the armies and roared out a challenge to the mighty Greek hero, Ajax. Ajax stepped forward and suggested that Hector stopped talking and ranting.

"We know what you want to do. We know well enough you want to fire our ships but we know how to fight. We will take your women, your gold and your city and plunder it."

As mighty Ajax spoke, an eagle flew high in the sky across the lines and over to the Trojan's city. It was a good omen and the Greek hordes roared with delight.

Hector called back at Ajax that he was all bluster, nothing more.

"Witless boasting never hurt anyone nor won battles. I promise you that when we burn your ships your body will fill the bellies of our war dogs and those black-eyed crows that wait beside all battlefields."

Hector raised his bronze-armoured arm and roared out to his men and they swept across the dusty earth. Battle commenced again.

Patroclus, Odysseus, Diomedes and Agamemnon led their men and the line held at the barricades. There were terrible losses on both sides. It was a desperate fight to hold the barricades. Some men were reduced to hurling rocks down on the Trojans as they tried to climb over the wall. The Trojan army fell back like a retreating tide and left behind a line of silent dead and screaming wounded.

They came on again and by sheer force of numbers began to force the Greeks back. But the Greek leaders pushed men into the weakest parts and fought like lions to keep the Trojans from breaking through. Then another part of the barricade came under threat and the Greek allies were forced to abandon it.

Zeus looked down from Olympus as King Priam looked down from the tower over the Scaean Gate. Helen named the bravest of the Greeks for him as she saw them in the press of battle. Ajax, Odysseus, Menelaus and Diomedes led their fighting men but the outcome was in the balance.

Hera saw that the Greeks were being forced back on to their ships. Then she saw the winning Trojans light flaming torches. Zeus refused to help Odysseus or Agamemnon or their men. Hera urged Poseidon to join in the battle but he was afraid of Zeus's warning not to interfere. Hera asked him again and he shook his mighty head and refused her once more. Hera offered to blind Zeus so that Poseidon could go down to the battlefield and help the Greeks. Reluctantly he agreed.

Hera dressed then in her softest robe, her most beautiful shoes, her hair adorned with pearls and silver. She perfumed herself with musk and poppy and came to her

husband. Zeus could never resist the beauty of his wife. Hera smiled and hid them both in a soft and pearly cloud. Zeus could see nothing of the battle down below now. Poseidon took his chance and with his help, the Greeks slowly pushed the flame-carrying Trojans back from the beach, back from the barricades and back on to the plain in front of the city gates.

Ajax slaughtered many Trojan heroes that day. Even great Hector was hurt and left the battlefield for the wound to be bound – he had escaped death for the moment. But the Trojan soldiers were dispirited to lose their mighty leader as Ajax sent even more of their men into the dark. One, Arxchelocus, son of Antenor, he struck with his spear at the point where neck and head and the last vertebra join. The spear tore out the sinews of his neck and he fell face down in the bloody earth, Ajax ripped out the spear and turned for more killing.

The battle still raged about the ships when Patroclus came to his friend Achilles who leaned against a boat and whittled a piece of driftwood. Patroclus begged to borrow his dearest friend's armour to lead his men into the battle and save the ships. Achilles still refused to fight but gave permission for his beloved friend to borrow his magnificent armour and to lead the wolf-wild Myrmidons, full of blood lust, into the fight.

So the mighty warrior Patroclus came into the battle dressed for all the world like the hero Achilles. And Hector returned to the fray, searching for men worthy to kill.

HECTOR AND PATROCLUS

Bodies lay now under a blanket of blood. As many men as flies round a butcher's block were fighting over the dead men to take their weapons and their armour. Some were hungry as wolves for more blood, more death. The gods tried to save their favourites and came in various disguises into the battle. Zeus was still with Hera under the cloud.

Hector became afraid and urged the Trojans to retreat to their city. Zeus began to watch the battle again and mused on the fate of Patroclus, who was doomed to die at Hector's hand. Patroclus turned to his men and urged them on against the running Trojans. Zeus had made him believe he was almost immortal. Patroclus was nearly at the gates of Troy when Zeus decided he would not be allowed to take the city and ordered Apollo to push Patroclus away. And so the Greek warrior fell back from the wall.

Around the field men slashed and thrust, screamed and roared and fell into the darkness while at the gates of Troy Hector was greeted by one who appeared to be his uncle, though it was really Apollo, son of Zeus, in disguise. His "kinsman" reminded him that running away was a cowardly act and unworthy of him, urging him to find Patroclus.

So Hector turned back into the melee of desperate, murderous men. He killed and slashed and thrust and raced about, at the same time searching for Patroclus. He found him and both warriors leapt from their bloody chariots. Patroclus took up a stone and hurled it at his enemy. Instead the stone hit Hector's charioteer. It struck the man's face and crushed his eyebrows into one, the bone cracked and his eyes fell into the dust and like a diver into the sea, he fell from the chariot and life left him.

Hector and Patroclus were parted by the thrust of the battle. Hector again went searching for his man. Patroclus, wounded by others in the fray, ripped an arrow from his body and fought on, despite the fact that Zeus had already doomed him to the dark.

Patroclus turned towards the Greek ships to find someone to bind his wounds when Hector found him. Patroclus had few weapons to defend himself by now. Hector struck the wounded Greek with his spear and drove it through his lower back. It was as if a lion had slaughtered a wounded boar. And Hector boasted then as the brave man died.

"Don't come back and try to fight me again, Patroclus, rider on horses. Nor see the fast ships... Don't try again to make me bleed as you are bleeding at my hand."

And before he fell into the darkness Patroclus told Hector that his fate was to die at the hands of mighty Achilles. Hector didn't listen. Standing with one foot on the dead man he held the shaft of his spear, pushed back and ripped it out. He bent to take his victim's armour.

And fast from the battlefield where Hector stripped the armour from the body of the brave Patroclus, news was brought to Achilles that his dearest friend had died at Hector's hand. For a moment the Greek leaned against the black-wood hull of his open boat and then he roared out one name.

"Hector!" And again he screamed the name – "Hector!"

BELOW *Archers, spearsmen and swordsmen fighting over the dead body of Patroclus.*

CHAPTER FOURTEEN

ACHILLES THE AVENGER

His dearest friend slain by Hector, the great wrath of Achilles, as invoked in the very first line of *The Iliad*, and which had caused the deaths of so many Greeks, was roused. He would re-enter battle and wreak his revenge.

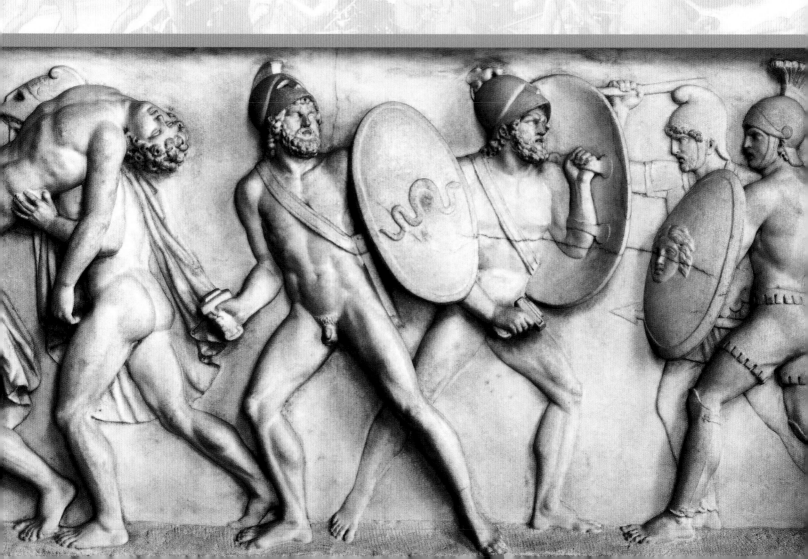

Achilles blamed himself for the death of Patroclus. In his grief, he called upon Thetis, his mother, who came to him from the depths of the sea. He told her that he had only ordered Patroclus to defend the ships from the firing torches the Trojans carried. Once they were pushed back his comrade should have returned to his camp, not challenged the mighty Hector. Achilles wept and his mother tried to comfort him, but only the death of the Trojan, Hector, would heal his pain.

Achilles took up the ashes from the fire and threw them over his head. He fouled himself with dirt and laid back his head and screamed to the skies. He promised the gods that he would have vengeance for the death of his friend. His tears streaked through the ashes on his face. Those about him feared for his mind, restraining him in case he tried to cut his own throat in his grief.

Thetis, who already knew that her son's fate was to die in battle, wept for Achilles. She reminded him that, despite his friend's death, Zeus had also given him what he desired – Agamemnon's army had suffered without his fighting prowess. Achilles agreed but told his mother it was a thin feast to receive for the wrong done to him. He was still angry with the High King for stealing Briseis from him and now he had also lost his beloved friend and many fine Greek comrades.

Achilles was determined to find Hector and slay him, as he would a wild boar. Thetis reminded her son that should he do so, he would die soon after, as fate had decreed. But fleet-footed Achilles didn't care. He begged his mother to ask the mighty Hephaestus, the great blacksmith, to make him more armour to replace that which Hector had ripped from the bloody body of Patroclus. Then he would go looking for his enemy and kill him. Thetis agreed, saying:

"Hector strides the battlefield and struts about in your armour with a horsetail plume in his helmet flying in the wind. He shall not be strutting there for long. In the morning, when the sun glitters on the sea I will be here with what you need."

Silver-footed Thetis left her son and went to Olympus to find Hephaestus.

Meanwhile, Hector stood on the killing field watching as the Sun sank into the sea. He listened as his friend, Polydamus, cautioned that the Trojans return into the city for the night. The next day, if Achilles should be given armour, Polydamus said, he would perhaps come out to fight and, if he did, many would descend into darkness and become fodder for vultures and dogs. But, though he sent some men back to defend the city, Hector ordered the Trojans to keep men in the field of battle. Troy was already protected by its mighty towers, high gate and huge timber barricades. At dawn they would put on their armour and wait. Hector declared:

"I will not run away from Achilles if he comes. Nor refuse the fight. I will meet him head to head and he or I will do something for which we shall be famous. The god of battles does not take sides in these matters and often he slays the slayer."

When they saw he was staying with them on the battlefield the Trojan soldiers cheered their champion. It was a foolish thing to do, for Athena, who loved the other side, had taken away Hector's common sense. The Trojans stayed in their ranks and waited for the dawn light.

BELOW *An oil painting by Maerten van Heemskerck showing Hephaestus handing Thetis the shield for Achilles.*

ARMOUR FOR ACHILLES

Silver-footed Thetis had wasted no time in getting to the brilliant, star-bright home of Hephaestus, the lame. It was a wonderful house, built by Hephaestus in bronze and gold. Thetis was greeted by his wife, who offered this rare guest food, but Thetis had no time to eat. The huge figure of Hephaestus came into the room and called out her name. He owed her his life and would do anything she requested. After putting his tools into a silver box, he wiped his face, hands and muscular neck with a sponge. He asked Thetis what brought her to his home.

Thetis told Hephaestus that she needed armour for Achilles. She begged him to help her aid the son she had raised.

"While he lives he is my light. He has to fight. He has to save the brave comrades and honour those who have already kissed the darkness. I beg you my friend, make him a breastplate and greaves for his legs, a sword and shield.

He is broken-hearted at the death of his friend. He has to fight in honour and needs weapons to do it."

Hephaestus took her hand and promised to create what she needed. He could not protect Achilles from the fate that was his, but he could make him the best of armour and the mightiest of swords. The great blacksmith turned to the fire and with bellows, pincers, hammers and pliers, he began. A blast of air blew into the melting vat and Hephaestus put bronze, tin and precious gold and silver into the roaring fire. As the metals melted he took up his mighty anvil, a heavy-headed hammer and great tongs to turn and lift and shape the metal. First he made a shield of three layers of bronze then a layer of bent oak planks and another of bronze again. Into the bronze he laid a design of silver and gold. He drew in the metal Earth, Heaven, the sea and all the star formations of the night sky. In glittering silver he also drew a city where men and women, brides and dancing boys turned and moved. He drew two armies in gold sitting in their own shining armour while their wives looked down from the city's mighty walls. He drew men fighting, some of whom were wounded and held by kind nymphs while others lay dead beneath the feet of their rearing horses. And there too, in copper and bronze, he drew farmers taking in the harvest and women washing their hair and their children.

Hephaestus poured his sorrow at the fate of men and women into his work. It was a shield in which Thetis could see all humankind – their lives and dreams and deaths were all played out on the mighty shield. It was a miracle of the blacksmith's art made for the sea-nymph's grieving son.

Then Hephaestus beat out a breastplate brighter than the white flames in the fire. He made a heavy helmet to fit close around the warrior's temples with a gold ridge to hold the horse's tail that was the sign of Achilles the fleet-footed.

Dawn was coming across the sea when Thetis took the armour. She came to Achilles who was still seated by his black-prowed ship and placed the armour before him. In the pale dawn an owl screamed and fell smothering its prey and slashing with its cruel, hooked beak. Thetis told her son to call to his Myrmidon comrades and go to Agamemnon to tell him he would fight. Achilles put on his magnificent armour. Patroclus would be avenged.

THE TIDE TURNS

Morning came and ate the shadows of the proud Greek ships along the beach. Light inched across the cold sand and the shadows of the mighty walls. Men stirred, blew light into their small fires and warmed their stiff, cold legs and hands. Each knew that, should he live, this was a day that would live in Greek minds forever.

The Greeks reached for their armour, for swords and shields, breastplates and helmets. Some watched as Achilles stood and prayed beside the funeral pyre of his dead friend Patroclus. He turned and asked the old fox, Odysseus, to honour his friend, so he sacrificed a lamb. Diomedes, who had been wounded, hobbled across using his spear as a crutch. Agamemnon came and watched brave Achilles as he stood in the early sunlight. The figures on his bronze and silver breastplate glinted, shone and shimmered across his god-made armour.

BELOW *A fresco painting from Pompeii that shows Briseis, the captive girl taken from Achilles by Agamemnon.*

"It is time this war was done," Achilles said. And Agamemnon made a signal to his servants. Then Briseis appeared, lovely as the morning, from the entrance of Agamemnon's tent. She approached Achilles as he stood in the sand below the prow of his ship and took his hand. Achilles smiled at Briseis and looked down into her grey eyes. The beautiful girl smiled up into his face. She touched the bronze breastplate, sparkling under the dawn light and asked him if he would fight again. Achilles replied that he must, as it was his destiny. He dismissed Briseis and strode across the sand to the fire where Agamemnon sat. The king turned to Achilles and said:

"Blinded by fate and the mighty Zeus, I made a mistake. The girl is yours and I return her untouched by any hand."

Achilles and Agamemnon made their peace and prepared for battle. In the morning light Achilles strode on to the plain before the Scaean Gate. Watching from the tower and from the length of the wall were the old men and the women of Troy. On the tower over the gates stood Priam and his family, among them Helen and Paris. Below stood the Trojan army in their companies. They saw the magnificent, solitary warrior standing before them. He looked across the lines of spears and shields and called out.

"It is time, Hector. It is time to face your fate. The mighty Achilles is come to the battlefield and one or other of us will slide into darkness before today is over. I will take your city. I will give your women as slaves to our men. I will take back the lovely Helen. I will offer the city to our men to run amok in. I will take your body and leave it for the carrion crows and the dogs of war. Hector… You killed my dearest friend, Patroclus. You shall go to your fate for that… if you have the courage. I will find you in the battle and we shall know our fate before the sun sinks."

Achilles turned then and walked back to his Greek comrades. Agamemnon took a black boar down to the seashore where he sliced its throat with his bronze-bladed sword and offered the bloody sacrifice to the gods. By now the army was roused. A thousand heads were bowed for a moment as the men put on their helmets. Broad-bladed battle spears glinted in the rising sun and shields glittered like ice. The men marched up the slopes, through the barricade and deployed on to the plain.

In Troy they could hear the marching feet and the thunder of sword on shield. Then they heard the roar of the war drums pounding like blood in the head and the rattle of chariots and galloping horses rolling over ground that would soon be slippery with the blood of the dead and wounded.

Achilles turned then as a chariot swerved across the plain, out of the Greek lines, towards him. He swung on to the back of the high-wheeled chariot like a dancer. He braced himself behind the driver against the gilded frame. Though carrying the weight of shield and sword he seemed to be as light as gossamer. The chariot raced along the length of the Trojan lines and back along the line of massed Greeks.

The Greek warriors raised their bronze swords and waited for the word like horses about to begin a race. Achilles stood tall in his chariot and when it stopped he turned to his men and roared:

"I know my fate. I will die on this place. But I will not turn back. I will give these Trojans their fill of bloody war… I will take Hector and feed him to the carrion birds… "

Odysseus, Diomedes, Ajax, Tydides, who was steady as a rock, and the sons of Nestor, Meriones and Idomeneus stood in the warming light and knew that today their fate was to be decided.

On Olympus the gods took their places to watch what was about unfold below the clouds around the mountain. Zeus, Athena, Hera, Aphrodite, Apollo and the other deities heard the silent prayers from the warriors of both sides and smelled the blood of the sacrificial animals slaughtered in the hope of victory by both sides. They listened to the whirr of the wheels of Achilles's chariot and the deep booming of swords beaten on the bronze bosses of the shields.

Achilles raised his sword arm and slashed down and the ranks began to move as one man. Spears levelled and shields in place, the lines of men moved slowly at first, gathering speed almost imperceptibly. The soldiers roared their battle cries – the business was now war.

From the high towering walls of the city Priam watched. He stood with his wife and saw the swaying mass of warriors hacking and stabbing, face to face, head to head and hand to hand. The king grieved to see the bravery of the warriors of both sides being squandered in death.

Across the plain the Sun flickered on the River Scamander and along its edge gulls waited. They were scavengers no less than the black crows sitting in the wind-blown trees closer to the city. The birds were no longer afraid of the sound of metal clashing on metal. No longer frightened by the screams of dying men and horses, no longer terrified by the thunder of a thousand men charging into the melee of spears and blades that faced them. These birds were carrion eaters and could bide their time until the sun went down and the two armies parted, for none of the men would fight in the darkness.

Priam watched his favourite son, Hector. He was a glory in gold-inlaid armour, his bronze sword covered to its hilt in blood, which also ran down his arm. The Greeks pressed forward and pushed the Trojans back against their sloping walls. Priam called down from the walls to urge his son to bring the Trojan forces back into the city, begging him to fight another day. For Achilles, who was roaring through the battlefield and coming ever closer in his unswerving search for Hector, the hero of Troy, had been blessed by the gods.

But Hector took no notice of his father and darted into the fray where his men were being pressed against the city walls. Knots of warriors swarmed about the bloody field, pushing, swaying and hacking at the enemy they found. Trojan or Greek, they were equal in bravery, skill and cruelty.

Priam called out again, pleading with Hector to return to the fortress city and comfort Andromache and his son. For Achilles was savage, and should he enter the walls of the city then the Trojans were doomed to death or slavery. For a moment Hector looked back and lifted his sword in salute to his father. He saw his brother's wife Helen looking about the battlefield for Paris, her husband.

The sun slid a little down the sky but the heat was still fierce. A cloud of dust lay over the sweating men as they went about their desperate business. Three chariots scythed across the plain with tremendous speed and archers fired their arrows from the back of them. One victim clutched at an arrow in his throat, another stared down for a moment at the feathers sticking out from his gut before he fell, twitched once and was across the Styx and gone. A third took an arrow in his eye, screaming and trying to tug the obscene thing free.

The chariots swung back across the battle and the drivers, targeted by flying spears, died still urging on their horses and screaming hate at their killers. Tangled in the reins they were dragged behind their horses like meat. They left a trail of blood across the battlefield and vanished across the plain towards the river.

The Trojans were held against the city walls. Archers in a tower along the wall fired down into the wild Greek hordes and some of the Trojan army crushed through the huge gates to safety. Achilles came roaring through the men locked in desperate and mortal battle.

Beside him Trojan warriors tried to hack his arms and back and an archer shot an arrow into the charging man's path. The arrow stuck in

Achilles's shield. Achilles was on the archer, slashed once and killed the man even as he ran on. He had seen Hector.

Priam called for Hector to run, for he saw that Achilles had a blood lust. Andromache put her hand on Priam's arm to stop him crying out again and begged him to leave Hector to his fate and not shame him in front of his young son. If he must fight and die here, it was his fate. Priam saw the passion in her face and the fear in her eyes. He bowed his head and was silenced.

Hector stood by the Scaean Gate and fought off the enemy warriors as the Trojan army hacked its way to safety behind the walls. A voice shouted his name across the tumult of battle. He looked across the mass of helmets, spears, swords and shields. He looked down the clattering lines of men. He looked past the arms slashing down and in and across and through with bloody swords. It was time.

Fate brought Hector and Achilles together as fate brought Heinrich Schliemann to a dusty hill in Turkey. Fate brought him to the city that been lost nine times already to earthquake, neglect, invasion, siege and savage war. Fate gave this man a vision so that Troy might live again. And with the city, Hector, Achilles and the characters of the ancient world could also live again.

BELOW *Hector and Achilles face each other on the battlefied. On the left the Greek ships can be seen, while Troy is on the right in the distance.*

CHAPTER FIFTEEN

THE NINE CITIES OF TROY

When Schliemann departed from the site at Hissarlik after the 1872 dig, he left behind a scene of destruction: rubble, deep trenches and even deeper pits scarred the site. Even by the standards of his time Schliemann had been ruthless in the manner in which he hacked his way into the site. But his only interest was to be acknowledged as the man who discovered Homer's Troy.

Schliemann was accused of vandalism and of doctoring his evidence to suit his theories. His reaction to such accusations was one of rage. He wrote wild, angry letters to professional journals and engaged in vicious correspondence with anyone who disagreed with him. Letters to the main newspapers of the time as well as to learned journals were filled with the bile he hurled indiscriminately at anyone who dared to question the value of what he was doing.

The fact is that the trench he dug across the whole site resulted in many ancient buildings being destroyed and artefacts of great archaeological importance were lost or carried away as rubbish. He had approached an archaeological site using mining techniques, engineers, pickaxes, spades and blocks and tackles in his all-consuming desire to discover the Troy of Priam and Hector. To Schliemann, these heavy-handed methods did not matter, for he believed he had found evidence that proved this was the site of ancient Troy.

LATER DIGS

More meticulous and well-trained archaeologists such as Wilhelm Dorpfeld, who had been Schliemann's assistant, Carl Blegen and Manfred Korfmann (see box overleaf) undertook later digs at Hissarlik. These expeditions revealed in more detail the succession of nine cities that had been built on the site.

Archaeologists long ago abandoned the "hack and dig" tactics of Schliemann. Now an important dig will have a team of experts using the best modern equipment, including image intensifiers, computers and metal detectors. Such work is no longer the province of an individual. International experts in such fields as pottery, metallurgy, climatology and forensics provide solutions to the questions thrown up by such a vast and important dig. It requires money, organization, patience and a willingness to seek the views and ideas of other experts.

Creating a fully realized picture of the life of the ancient inhabitants of the hill at Hissarlik had been of no interest to Schliemann, who had wanted spectacular discoveries. He had believed that at the level of Priam's Troy he would find them. *The Iliad* mentions spectacular armour and weapons and Helen's wealth, which Schliemann took to mean gold and jewels. Homer and Virgil describe Priam's palace as having a vast number of rooms where the extended royal family lived. Schliemann had been certain that when he reached the level of "mighty Ilium" there would be magnificent finds and that these objects would show the world that he was a better scholar and a better archaeologist than any academic who had disputed his claims. He had to find something magnificent, which he certainly did.

Modern archaeology, however, is not so singular. It does not rely on finding gold and statuary, precious stones and magnificently painted amphorae. Instead it aims to provide a picture of the lives of the people who inhabited an ancient site. To do this means dealing with seemingly mundane and humdrum finds. This would have been an alien prospect to Schliemann.

Through the research and the information that forensic experts provide it is now possible to detail even the dietary habits of ancient people. Forensic work on bones that were found at Troy indicated that deer, pigs and fish featured heavily in the diet of the inhabitants. Goat meat no doubt was also on the menu, as it still is in the region.

OPPOSITE *The ruins of Troy, with an example of a reconstruction. Note the well in the foreground.*

CARL BLEGEN

In 1892 and 1893, Wilhelm Dorpfeld made some important advances at Hissarlik. His work was taken up in 1932 when the University of Cincinnati sent a team to the site under Carl Blegen (1887–1971), a highly skilled archaeologist. He worked on the Hissarlik site for seven years, during which his systematic methods unravelled much of the chaos that Schliemann's digging methods had left behind.

It was Blegen who confirmed what Dorpfeld had believed, which was that the level of the true site of Troy was Troy 7a. According to the evidence, the city at this level was destroyed by fire at about the traditional date of the Trojan War. This city is two levels above the one that Schliemann proclaimed was Priam's city.

MANFRED KORFMANN

Manfred Korfmann of the University of Tübingen in Germany has been actively involved with digging the Hissarlik site since 1988. Since then, he has widened the area of excavation in order to see what lay outside the inner walls. It is his work that has begun to show that the city was much larger than at first thought.

He has built on the belief that Troy was a wealthy and important trading centre. There were, he discovered, many houses built outside the fortified walls. The people beyond the walls would have been farmers, artisans and workers for the inner city. At a time of invasion, those who lived outside would have been able to withdraw into the safety offered by the walls.

When, in 2001, Professor Korfmann released his findings and presented a model of the city he believed had been built around the central mound, he couldn't have predicted the controversy it unleashed. It was the sort of controversy that Schliemann would have found familiar.

One of Korfmann's colleagues, an ancient historian called Professor Kolb, compared him to Eric von Daniken, the author of books about extraterrestrial visitations. Professor Kolb claimed that Troy was at best "at the margins of civilization…" and not the hub of a trading empire. These statements drew support for Korfmann from two English colleagues who wrote to *The Times* stating that they were both appalled at the intemperate language of Professor Kolb, who had written that "his [Korfmann's] interpretations distort the evidence".

Professor Korfmann and his supporters continue to hold to their view, which is supported by current excavations. However, nothing, it seems, changes in the critical hothouse that is academia – nothing – that is but the names.

Plants and seeds, which have survived in the houses or that have been caught in the clay of the pots as they were made, can be studied so that the grains grown can be identified. This helps to analyse not just diet, but also the climate of the time. Carbon dating technology helps put a more accurate timeframe on the various layers at a site such as Troy, as does the comparison of pots discovered in the various excavations at the site with pots from the surrounding region. Forensic work away from the site, in universities and specialized institutions, for example, can offer more and more understanding of ancient sites such as Troy. Technology offers the scholar/archaeologist answers to many questions it was not possible to answer when Schilemann dug. Hand-crafted items such as bone needles, spinning wheels, loom weights, metalwork, jewellery, pottery figures and weapons provide valuable clues, not only about the life lived in the various cities that were built on the site, but also about connections between Troy and the rest of the ancient world between 3000BC and AD600.

The reasons for the end of one city and the beginning of another are found in a number of ways. The condition of the soil between the layers is one factor, as is evidence of fire, for example in plaster that has been baked bright red. A jumble of huge stones mixed into the building blocks of houses may indicate an earthquake, while arrowheads, javelins and hastily concealed treasures indicate invasions and sieges. In the case of the top layer, and most recent city, economics may have reduced this once important trading centre to an unimportant hamlet.

This final stage in the life of a settlement is the point at which nature takes over again. The hill of Hissarlik was returned to the forces of the Earth and the elements, which caused the buildings to disintegrate. Dust blown up across the plain covered the hillside and provided a foothold for brambles and bushes. Hissarlik became a small mound in a river plain.

It took Schliemann and his belief that by using clues in *The Iliad* as a map he would find the site to discover Troy. It took later archaeologists to evaluate the layers of the city and indeed to discover what is probably the true site of Priam's Troy. It is ironic that the level that Schliemann declared to be Priam's city was not in fact correctly dated. He was too eager to be famous to take the time to bring the scholarship and rigour to bear on the cities that he burrowed through. Those cities have provided rich territory for the scholars who came after him and they continue to do so.

BELOW *Gold and silver earrings, silver armrings, gold rings, copper nails, tools and other artefacts, which were dicovered at the digs at Hissarlik.*

THE LEVELS OF TROY

TROY 1 *c.*3000–2500BC

The hill that is the site of the cities stands on a rocky outcrop at the end of a low ridge. Before digging began it stood 32 metres (100 feet) over the plain. Much of the mound was made from the debris of a number of cities. Troy 1, which was at the bottom of the mound, was surrounded by a rough stone wall. A short segment of the wall still stands as does some of the main gate, which was flanked by two square towers. This outer wall is about two-and-a-half metres (eight feet) thick.

The remains of the foundations of some houses at this level are still contained in Schliemann's trench. At first these were thought to be single rooms with entrance halls very similar to early Greek temples. But in 1988, digs led by Manfred Korfmann cleared the trench and found that they were rows of narrow alternating foundations built of mud brick on stone and were not free-standing.

There is evidence of infant burial in one of the houses. A shallow pit was scraped out and a flat stone covered the body. No adult burials have been found within the central area of the city. There may have been a belief that if a new-born child died it still required protection and so was buried close to its parents.

The inhabitants of Troy 1 were of the Early Bronze Age. They made tools from copper, stone or the bones of animals that they had hunted. They used clay pots made by the coil technique and not on a wheel. Women would have used pottery spindles and loom weights to spin thread and then weave cloth. Evidence suggests that Troy 1 was destroyed by fire.

TROY 2 *c.*2500–2300BC

This level was enclosed in walls that at 110 metres (300 feet) were twice the diameter of Troy 1. The defensive wall had a broadly sloping outer face, which meant that it was better able to withstand earthquakes. Above this a layer of sun-dried brick supported by the stones of the wall. This wall made a sophisticated line of defence with small towers a few metres apart. Over the two main gates a tower jutted out from the wall. There were large covered passages under the towers and timbers supported the corridors.

The roads to the gateways were made of steeply laid limestone slabs. There were other entrances apart from the main gate. Some of them led on to cobbled yards within the walls. The houses were more sophisticated than in Troy 1 and it is clear that the inhabitants within the walls lived a life of relative luxury. The ruler of this Troy probably lived in the palace and the fine houses grouped within the walls housed his retinue. Artefacts found indicate a sophisticated society. Work in bronze, gold, and silver was of a very high quality and the potters, now using the wheel, were making beautiful jars and bowls and delicate two-handled containers for wine.

Because he found evidence of such wealth here, Heinrich Schliemann believed that this level was Homer's Troy. He was wrong. Troy 2 was burned down by invaders.

TROY 3 *c.2300 – 1700*BC

It appears that survivors stayed and rebuilt the town after invasion, probably following a similar way of life to those who inhabited Troy 2. Some of the invaders may have stayed and rebuilt with the indigenous people or they may have looted and burned Troy 2 before moving on and leaving the local people to salvage what they could.

TROY 4 AND 5

These were each bigger than Troy 2 and 3, but life in this settlement did not change radically as far as we can tell from what little evidence remains after Schliemann's ruthless techniques at the site.

TROY 6 *c.1700–1250*BC

Rebuilt again in the Middle Bronze Age, the central part of the city was a large acropolis, surrounded by strong walls and elegant houses with wooden pillars supporting the stone roofs. Wooden rooms were built on top of these, creating two-tier buildings. The approach to the eastern gateway is a two-metre (six-foot) wide passage between walls. At the end of the corridor the passage turns sharply inward to a wooden door. This turn in the passage made the entrance very easy to protect from invaders.

Much of the top level of Troy 6 was cut down by the later inhabitants of the Hellenistic and Roman periods. Before that, the walls were enlarged with large towers. One of these was built as an observation tower dominating the acropolis and looking out over the land beyond the walls. The tower also enclosed a cistern. This cistern and a well in a courtyard provided a safe water supply if the city was besieged. This city provided a safe refuge for the outlying citizens in times of emergency.

The black and grey Minoan pottery found in Troy was probably brought to the city from Crete or other parts of the Hellenic world as trade. It should not be forgotten that the site of Troy commands a powerful position overlooking the Bosporus. The rulers of the city could have controlled much of the shipping that passed through those straits, and may have taken tolls from all who passed. This was as good a reason as the beauty of Helen for outsiders to try and control the city.

In one part of the wall a gateway has been discovered that was later blocked up with uncut stones. Could this be the gate through which the Wooden Horse was dragged? There was a large gateway to the south of the city with a broad street of limestone blocks leading to it. Could this have been the Scaean Gate in front of which Achilles

TROY 7A *c*.1250–1180BC

This level was rebuilt after an earthquake and is therefore a direct continuation of the city at the lower level. The population rebuilt part of the great protective wall and a new wall was added on the eastern side.

The road running down to the southern and main gate had an underground drain that ran along its centre to take rainwater from the upper part of the city. The houses built along this road were less elegant than some of those found in earlier levels. They were built very much closer together, which could be an indication that people moved into the city from the surrounding countryside because they were afraid of regular raids.

Almost every house had vast storage jars set deeply in the ground and closed with a heavy stone slab. These jars were used to store grain, olives, oil and wine for use in emergencies. This was a city under constant threat, which explains why spear- and arrowheads and human remains are found at this level. The fact that the human remains were not buried indicates a violent invasion of the city. Added to the fact that this level of Troy was destroyed by fire there is enough evidence to convince that Level 7/7a is Homer's city.

TROY 7B c.1180–1000BC

The siege was over. The Greeks had left and the destroyed city was reoccupied by a few survivors who then began to drift away. Maybe after so many invasions, earthquakes and fires people believed Troy was a city of ill omens.

TROY 8 *c.*1000–85BC

This level shows evidence of a typical Greek colonial style. As a Greek settlement, Troy's culture changed, and areas for religious observance and sacrifice were built near the acropolis. It is claimed that when Xerxes, the Persian king, was on his way to invade mainland Greece in 480BC he came here and sacrificed a thousand oxen to the Greek gods as a bribe. He then built a bridge of boats across the Dardanelles. The Greek gods responded to his sacrifice by destroying the bridge in the strong current that swept through the straits.

Alexander the Great came here on his way to the battle of Granicus and made sacrifice to the goddess Athena in 334BC. He took from the walls of the temple armour he believed to have been that of the hero he claimed as one of his ancestors, Achilles. However, despite these important visitors, the city continued to decline. The last time it had any real importance was with the arrival of the Romans.

TROY 9 c.85BC–AD600

The Romans had a special interest in settling in Troy, as it was from here, after the sack and pillage of the city by the Greeks, that their founding father Aeneas escaped from the flames of the city. It is a story movingly recorded in Virgil's *Aeneid*.

Various emperors came to the city, which they improved with temples and other civic buildings such as a theatre, a stadium, an aqueduct and baths. They also left many mosaics.

The Romans felt strongly that the city should be preserved. Emperor Constantine the Great decided to build a new capital for the Roman Empire in the east and even thought that he might choose Troy as its site. He then chose not to, building in Byzantium, now known as Istanbul, which overtook Troy as the focus for trade across the Roman Empire.

CITY OF LEGEND

The nine levels confirm that Hissarlik was a major settlement for a long period of time. It contained the ruins of a city that had suffered siege and invasion at the time the myths about the siege were being told. It is a tribute to Schliemann's unshakeable belief in himself and dogged determination to follow the clues in the story of Troy as written down by Homer, that the site was rediscovered. Schliemann may have been hard nosed, aggressive, rude, selfish and overbearing but, in the end, it is due to him that the city was brought back to the light.

The treasures he found may not have been worn by Helen of Troy and they may never have been seen by Priam or Paris but they were the bait that drove him to the discovery that began the modern history of archaeology. The story of *The Iliad* touches even now a dark, mythological past with glimmers of light. It opens to anyone who hears, reads or sees the story a connection to ancient heroes and ancient gods, to life and death, to honour and to sacrifice.

This story of the death of heroes has been told for three thousand years and for three thousand years Achilles has taken his revenge on Hector.

OPPOSITE *A stone amphitheatre at Level 9, the top level, which was associated with the Roman occupation of Troy.*

BELOW *A map of Troy created from the information discovered by the digs through the various levels.*

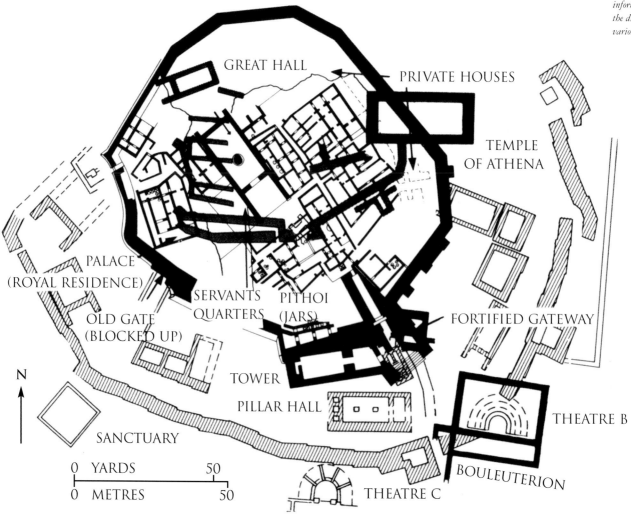

GREAT HALL

PRIVATE HOUSES

TEMPLE OF ATHENA

PALACE (ROYAL RESIDENCE)

SERVANTS QUARTERS

PITHOI (JARS)

FORTIFIED GATEWAY

OLD GATE (BLOCKED UP)

N

TOWER

PILLAR HALL

THEATRE B

SANCTUARY

0 YARDS 50

0 METRES 50

BOULEUTERION

THEATRE C

CHAPTER SIXTEEN

A BLOODY DUEL

The story of the siege of Troy, as told by Homer, builds to its climax with the meeting between its two great heroes: the Trojan Hector and the Greek Achilles.

Fate ran towards Hector in the shape of Achilles, the horse runner. Hector knew of the strength of the Greek, but feared more to be called a coward than he feared death, which he knew must come. The sun blazed across the dark red plain, lighting the bronze and gold, the blades of swords and tips of lances. His armour glinting as the lowering rays struck his breastplate, Achilles ran towards the Trojan, looking as if he was engulfed in flames.

Looking down from Troy Priam cried out for his son. The battle between the armies slowed and stopped and the men watched as the gap between the two heroes closed. Achilles ran through the lines of battle, past dead men piled on other dead men and past the dying dropping into darkness. Then Hector turned and ran. It was a calculated act as he knew that Achilles was not battle-hardened. He had been out of the fight for so long that Hector thought he could wear out his enemy by making him chase him. Then, when the Greek was exhausted, he could turn on him and take him down. Achilles, laughing, raised his spear and ran after Hector.

Once round the walls of the city the two men ran. The ground was rough and pitted with foxholes and rocks. If either were to stumble or fall he would last no longer than it took the other to pounce and send him to the Styx. With each step, Achilles gained ground. Hector had forgotten that Achilles could outrun horses. But Hector had no choice – fate had made a decision.

Hector ran past the southern gate of the city. He did not look up into the face of his silent wife, Andromache, nor at his baby son. Twice around the city and Hector was breathless. He carried his sword, spear, helmet and shield and, although he was strong, they were a terrible burden.

Athena came to Achilles and told him it was time to stand and fight. Achilles stopped before the Scaean Gate and paused for breath, as instructed by the goddess. Looking up he saw Priam staring down into his eyes. He lifted his spear in salute to the king.

Athena then went to Hector and told him too that it was time to confront fate and fight. Hector had stopped running and was breathing deeply as he tried to still his heart. He looked up and saw the line of black willows bent by the wind that forever howled across the plain. He saw the glint of the river and, beyond that, the sea. He smelt the acrid aroma of fresh blood on his sword and over his arms and legs. His heart pounded like a drum of war. The curving wall of the city swept away from him. He looked to where the mighty Achilles stood and saw the flat black eyes of death staring at him. He was a spear throw from his enemy. Fate had arrived.

THE FIGHT

Before the bloody duel began, Hector asked something of his enemy.

"Before we fight can we agree that whoever wins will treat the corpse of his enemy with respect and will not throw it to the dogs for food. I swear I will only take your armour, as is the custom, and then will give you to your men unsullied. Will you do the same for me?"

Achilles spoke so softly then to Hector.

"You're a bigger fool than I thought. I won't rest until your blood floods the gates of Troy. You killed my best friend. I would eat my mother's heart before I'd agree to what you ask. I'd eat your raw flesh. When I have killed you your body will be left at the foot of these walls. Our war dogs will eat well. You'll have no burial and no sacrifices. You will be gutted in view of your own father and your wife and son, I promise you that."

Achilles leaned back a little and hurled the first of his spears at Hector. It missed the Trojan. Hector mocked the other whose arms were bloodied to the shoulders and whose face was a mask of cold fury. Furious and taunting, Hector launched his own spear.

About them men leaned on swords and lances and drew breath. They watched as the two men circled each other looking for an opening. Those who saw this duel knew they were seeing two of the greatest living warriors and that only one of them could survive. It would be a tale to tell their grandchildren. Priam, too, knew that this would be a great battle, but like all conflicts between such men it would end in blood on the ground. As the king looked down and heard the groans of wounded men across the battlefield, there were tears in his eyes, for Achilles, son of Thetis, was invincible.

Hector's spear went straight enough to hit Achilles's shield; it bent on the bronze boss and Achilles shrugged it aside. He was not hurt and he had another spear. Hector had none and had no choice but to draw his bronze-bladed sword and to charge.

Achilles used his shield to stop Hector finding the mark with his sword. The blade sliced into the edge of the shield and cut the leather rim. Hector feinted high for the face and at the last moment swung low for the groin of the mighty Achilles. Wherever he tried to place his sword Achilles parried it with the shield. Hector had to stay close so that Achilles had no room to use his spear. He charged in again, and again Achilles brushed aside the sword. Then, as Hector closed in, Achilles took aim with his bronze-headed spear. He had seen an opening between Hector's shield and the edge of his helmet where it covered his neck.

THE DEATH OF A TROJAN HERO

It was Hector's speed that killed him. As he ran in to attack again he skewered himself on Achilles's spear. The Greek stepped back, lowered the point and forced Hector down, writhing, twitching and curling about the spear that pinned him through his throat to the bloody ground. Achilles leaned down on the spear until his face was close to the choking man.

RIGHT *A relief carved on an altar which shows the battle between Hector and Achilles goes on.*

"I promised that you would feed the dogs. I will leave you for the carrion birds to pull your guts out. I will leave you naked for the foxes and rats, the owls and the rest. My friend Patroclus will burn on his pyre with all reverence to the gods while you are dishonoured."

Hector, choking on the spear shaft, begged Achilles

to be merciful and let his father Priam pay ransom for his body but Achilles, full of hate, laughed in his face. Hector begged once more, this time asking that his wife and mother could honour him when dead. But Achilles, to his shame, laughed in Hector's face again.

Hector reminded his killer that one day he would also die. He prayed that the gods would not forget what Achilles did to Hector, son of Priam, King of Troy. And then he died. But the shame went on for Achilles. He took the armour of the dead man, then called his charioteer to join him. Achilles then slit Hector's ankles, pushed a leather thong through them and lashed his body to the axle of his chariot so that it dragged on the bloody earth. Then Achilles drove the chariot around the city walls.

Priam and the Trojan nobles of the city stood on the walls of the city and watched, appalled at such sacrilege. The body was flayed as it dragged across the stones. Hector's head and face, which thudded over the sand and stones, were obliterated. And when Achilles stopped, the Greek warriors ran to marvel at the Trojan champion. They kicked and abused the naked hero, spat on him, thrust swords and spears into his dead body. It was shameful.

BELOW *Achilles dishonours the corpse of the dead Hector. The gods will not be pleased.*

The next day brought more of the same behaviour, as Achilles let the mighty Priam watch the dishonour he did to his son's body. He let the dead man's wife see how he abused this brave man. In his arrogance and anger he let Hector's baby son see his father's dishonour. The gods were not pleased by this arrogance. It was no man's place to dishonour a good and brave and decent man, such as Hector was, in such a way. For this shameful behaviour Achilles would pay.

From the tower on the Trojan wall, Andromache let loose a wild ululation of pity and grief. Her husband had not been properly washed and prepared for that final journey all men must take. She unpinned her hair and knelt on the ground below the tower where she scratched up soil from the ground and poured it over her head. She raked her face with her nails and tore the flesh into bloody streaks as she cried out:

"I will burn the grave clothes we keep in scented chests at home. You will be naked and I will have no protector and your son will have no father."

Again and again she tore up the earth and poured it over her head.

The Sun set and Achilles sat once more beside his ship, sated with blood and vengeance. His men did not look at him.

THE GODS INTERVENE

At night, Aphrodite hid Hector's bloody body under a perfumed cloud so that dogs and carrion birds could not dishonour this brave man further. In the morning a sea mist covered the plains below the walls of mourning Troy. On Olympus, Apollo was wild with anger at the treatment of his favourite, Hector. He shouted at Hera when she tried to persuade Zeus that Achilles had not meant to shame the Trojan hero. Apollo was disgusted that no sacrifices had been made, no rites had been said, and that the body had not been washed. Only Aphrodite's intervention had saved Hector's body from the scavengers. Achilles, Apollo demanded, should be punished.

Hera tried to defend Achilles but Zeus turned on his wife in anger. He was also disgusted by the disrespect Achilles had shown Hector. He commanded Thetis to tell her son to offer the body to Priam so that he could pay a ransom and honour his son's body as custom decreed. He also told Thetis to remind Achilles that his time on Earth was short, and that he would soon need the gods on his side. Hera still protested, but Zeus, the thunder maker, roared across Olympus and down across the sea and his wife was quiet. Thetis did what was commanded of her.

At first Achilles argued with her but then Thetis pointed out Zeus's rage and across the dark sea, a flicker of lightening lit the sky and thunder roared. Achilles agreed to do what had to be done.

In the city Priam told his family that he was going down into the enemy camp to ask Achilles to let him have back the body of his dearest son. They all told him he was mad and that Achilles might kill him too but Priam rounded on them, saying that he would rather die than never hold his son again. He turned to Paris and ordered him to fill an ox cart with golden treasure and then to get out of his sight.

Before he left for the Greek camp Priam made a libation to the gods. As the Sun was sinking across the sea he strode into the tent where Achilles was feasting. He knelt and kissed the hands that had the blood of his son on them and asked him to think of his own father and to honour him for coming to take away the body of his son. Achilles, astonished at the courage of the old man, lifted him from his knees and asked him to take wine. Achilles refused the riches Priam had brought and returned the body of his brave son for the funeral rites.

Patroclus, the beloved friend of Achilles, was burned before the Trojan gates while Hector was washed and perfumed and then taken for burning too. Libations were made on both sides. Hector's bones were placed in an ivory and gold box wrapped in purple cloth. It was placed in a stone-lined hole and covered with a huge flagstone over which they piled a huge mound and left a guard there to protect it from any enemy who might come to desecrate it.

So ended the life of Hector, master of horses. And after the libations and the funeral rites were done, the war between the Greeks and Trojans began again. Achilles took his chariot and rode towards Troy at the head of the Greek army while Zeus warned Thetis that her son had little time to live.

OPPOSITE *Painted by Aleksander Ivanov (1806–58), this image depicts Priam, as he begs Achilles for the return of his son's body so that it may be prepared for burial.*

CHAPTER SEVENTEEN

THE WOODEN HORSE

◆◆

The Iliad ends with Hector's funeral and with the death of Achilles foretold.
However, the story of Troy doesn't end there, as the fate of Achilles and the end
of the War, were re-told by storytellers, and alluded to by Homer in his other
great work, *The Odyssey*. Virgil takes up the story in the *Aeneid*.

THE DEATH OF ACHILLES

Their greatest champion gone, the Trojans sent for reinforcements while on the beach the Greeks cooked meat on skewers, wrestled, sharpened battle-blunted weapons and waited for the next battle. They watched the gates of Troy for any excursion by their warriors. Achilles was away, raiding along the coast when a challenge came. From the gates of the city came Memnon of Ethiopia, who challenged the Greeks to put up a champion to fight him in single combat. Ajax of a thousand battles stood up to fight.

Memnon, a huge man, wore a black-maned helmet. His breastplate was made of bronze and he carried a long lance and huge sword. As the two men faced each other on the killing ground, Achilles raced back across the plain. Before the fight had begun, Achilles asked Ajax to leave Memnon for him, for it was he who had killed his friend, the son of Nestor.

Hiding behind the shields of the Trojans lurked Paris, whom Achilles did not see. He carried his curved bow of ibex horn and his quiver of arrows was full. He moved behind the Trojan shields unseen by the enemy. All eyes were on the single combat that was about to begin. Paris chose a long-flighted arrow. There was danger for Achilles from all sides.

Achilles flung his spear at Memnon and Apollo nudged the flying death aside. Paris checked his arrow and put it to the string of the curved bone bow. Then Memnon leaned back and holding his lance high over his head hurled it. The lance flew past

Achilles's head and buried itself in the ground nearly halfway up its shaft. As the two men circled each other both looked for a weakness in their opponent. Paris still watched from behind the shields and waited, his arrow on his bow. He was ready to avenge his brother, Hector.

Memnon began to move towards Achilles who feinted right and left and then levelled the blade he held. The huge Ethiopian ran at Achilles but at the same moment, the Greek lunged forward, aiming his bronze blade. It hit Memnon low down between the breastplate and his armoured belt. Memnon could not draw back. He dropped as fast as a well-slaughtered bull. Achilles turned away in triumph. He had killed another great Trojan hero.

At that moment Paris let loose his arrow, aiming it at the one place that Thetis had not covered when she dipped her child in the River Styx. The bronze-tipped arrow smashed into Achilles's heel and killed him. Apollo could not protect his favourite against fate Achilles looked into the darkness and was gone.

A SOLUTION TO THE SIEGE

With the great Achilles dead, Agamemnon lost the will to fight. He suggested to his generals that they end the decade-long siege and return home, without recapturing Helen. But a goddess may have whispered a plan to one of the Greeks. Odysseus, the fox, told the world, when he returned to Ithaca, that it was his idea. By then, there was no one left to say he lied, but he was always a boaster. Others said it was the idea of Panopeus. Whoever it was who whispered, Agamemnon listened. And because he listened, the mighty walls of Troy were breached.

The idea was simple. The only way to beat the Trojans was to get inside the walls of the city. It was obvious and had been for ten years. Odysseus explained that all they had to do was listen and then to do exactly as he suggested. His comrades agreed.

The Greeks gathered all the wood they could find. Then, out of sight of the walls, they built a huge, hollow, wooden horse. It stood on a platform and they rolled it from the beach to the plain in front of the Scaean Gate. It was dark when the Greeks put the horse in place. Their long ships waited in the water, seams caulked, stores in place and sails mended, each one anchored in the still sea by a stone. The men who had rolled the huge horse into place hurried back to the shore and all, except one, joined the crews of the ships. Quietly the fleet sailed into the darkness while the horse remained on the beach with its own cargo. The one man who remained had been chosen because he was the best liar in the besieging army.

The morning was pearl bright and when the guard on the Trojan wall looked out across the plains towards the sea he dared not believe his eyes. There was no sign of the Greek army or their ships. Nothing remained except smouldering fires and the rubbish and detritus of the ten-year-long siege. Seagulls flocked about the debris, tugging at the carcasses of animals left there. They pecked at old clothes, broken cooking pots and torn sandals. Crows hopped and pecked about the pyres on which the bones of recently killed men had been burned. There was no sight of the besiegers. The Trojan guard listened but he could hear nothing but the distant hiss of waves sucking at the pebbles. Then he saw the mighty shape of a horse standing where once had stood the altar of the gods.

He called to his comrades. Soon they lined the city walls, staring at the horse. Then Priam came and looked across the plain on which his son had been slaughtered such a

ABOVE *Epeios, inspired by the goddess Athena, works on the Trojan Horse. Detail from a bronze mirror of the late fourth century BC.*

short time before. He looked across the dusty land and saw where the invincible Achilles had fallen. As Trojans looked from the walls and saw no sign and heard no sound of those enemy warriors they sent thanks to their beloved Athena.

Aeneas, the only mighty hero left within the city walls, came and stood on the tower. Leader of the Dardanian allies, he had taken refuge with his people inside the walls of Troy when Achilles had raided his land on the wooded slopes of Mount Ida. At the time his father, the Dardanian king Anchises, had refused to take the side of Troy or of the Greeks. Because of that, when he came with Aeneas to the city their cousin Priam had treated them coldly though he welcomed the reinforcements who came with them.

For the ten years of the siege Aeneas had been snubbed by the Trojan King Priam. Despite this, he had fought against many Greek heroes; Diomedes, Idomeneus and even mighty Achilles. Twice the gods had rescued him from certain death. Aeneas was respected by those who knew him well. He was honoured as a deeply religious family man. He cared for his lame and elderly father, loved his wife Creusa and adored his little son, Ascanius.

Now he stood apart a little and looked down at Andromache, widow of Hector, as she slowly mounted the stone steps to the top of the wall.

"It's done," he said. "If they have gone. If they have left us alone at last. My father and my wife and I can go home perhaps."

Holding her son in her arms, Andromache, streaked with earth and blood, nodded. She had nowhere else to go and no one to go with. Aeneas touched her hand and the boy's head and remembered, as she did, her mighty husband being dragged face down behind the chariot of Achilles. Priam nodded at Aeneas and turned his back.

The sun rose a little higher. The weeds by the edge of the water began to dry and to smell of rot. The siege of Troy was done. All that was left was the huge wooden horse standing on the plain, silent and still.

Priam and his warriors opened the gates of the city. For the first time in ten years the men, women and children of the mighty city could walk freely across the dust and down to the long beach. The children began to tear off their clothes. They ran across the weed and through the nibbling little waves at the edge of the sea, jumping and shouting into the darker water. Priam forgot his sorrows for a moment and smiled. Turning, he walked along the beach to where the horse stood.

Surrounded by the wild shepherds who had captured him a figure stood beside the horse.

Unarmed, un-armoured and seeming lost, the man stood there and watched as the king walked slowly towards the horse. The man told Priam that his name was Sinon and that he was a Greek. He went on to tell the king that he was there because the seer, Calchas, had condemned him as a sacrifice to Apollo. He explained that if the Trojans were to kill him, it would bring happiness to those who hated him – Odysseus, Agamemnon and Menelaus. He explained to the Trojan king that the Greek army had long wanted to return to their homes and that when Achilles died, they had lost heart completely. Sinon told how he was prepared for sacrifice with perfumed oils and garlands. Around him the Trojan army listened with bated breath as Sinon spun the tale of his escape and of Greek fear:

"I broke my ropes and hid amongst the marsh reeds. I'd given up hope of going home. Now I wish a curse on all those men who'd have had me sacrificed to placate

the gods. It was all because their priest and that fox Odysseus hated me. The gods hate them for their sacrilegious acts. Pallas Athena has abandoned the Greeks because Odysseus touched a sacred priestess with bloody hands. Calchas, the priest, is afraid. He told them they had to risk the stormy waves and go home to be cleansed of their sin. They will come back. Calchas advised them to build this mighty horse in the name of Pallas Athena. It had to be so big that it could not be taken into the city.

"Calchas said that if it was received with simple piety Athena would favour those who took the horse. So it is too big to take through the city gates. If you did take it into Troy then all the powers of Asia would come to your aid and destroy the enemies of Troy. Calchas saw that in the entrails of the last sacrifice he made on the shore."

Sinon sighed then and looked away to sea with tears in his eyes. And the Trojans believed Sinon, who was the greatest liar in the whole host of the Greek hordes. In this way, the liar baited the trap.

The Trojans were determined to take the horse into their city; riches had been promised if they only they could get it into the walls. The Trojan high priest, Laocoon, came down from the city and urged his compatriots to burn the horse where it stood, but they did not listen. The priest made an offering to the great god Poseidon, slaughtering a black bull by the sea. Laocoon turned then and shouted at the Trojans on the beach.

"Do you believe the Greeks will sail away and leave you gifts? They have a reason. Listen to your priest. Do not trust any Greek, not even when they come to you with a gift."

If they had listened to their priest then Troy's mighty walls would still be there and Priam would still be the king. But except for Aeneas, who thought the priest spoke sense, the Trojans chose not to listen. The sacrifice over, Laocoon and his two sons washed their bloody hands in the sea. As they bent to the waves two huge serpents slithered from the water, coiled about the boys and ate them. Laocoon attacked the slavering serpents but they wound twice around his body. He hacked their twisting bodies with his sword but, bleeding black blood and bile, the serpents crushed him and slithered away.

The Trojan people shuddered at what they had seen and blamed their dead priest for what he had said about the sacred horse, the symbol of Poseidon. Now they were desperate to take the horse into the city. Some knocked a hole in the mighty walls and others took tree trunks and rolled the huge horse slowly into the city.

It was the last day of a doomed people and they spent their time dressing the altars about the city and raising prayers to the gods. They hung wreaths of victory about the mighty neck of the Wooden Horse. Unmarried boys and virgins sang and hauled on the ropes that dragged the horse across the broken wall. Inside the belly was a clash as of bronze falling on bronze. But the Trojans heard nothing above the noise of the songs and the prayers.

The horse slipped easily on the wide, paved road into the centre of the city.

No one listened as the soothsayer, Cassandra, daughter of Priam, foretold of death and blood running down the gutters of the city. She was never to be believed. If only the Trojans had listened.

And night came. Sinon, no prisoner but a garlanded guest slipped away from the celebrations through the empty streets of the city. He came to the square where the horse stood under the starlight. No one watched as he did what had been planned. Troy was doomed.

CHAPTER EIGHTEEN

THE FALL OF TROY

◆ ◆

The Greeks had set their trap. The Wooden Horse was inside the walls of Troy, and the city was about to fall to its ruin.

ANCHISES AND APHRODITE

Anchises, the father of Aeneas, had been visited by Aphrodite, disguised as an ordinary but lovely girl. Anchises had fallen in love with her and she had a son by him, Aeneas. Aphrodite swore him to silence about the boy, who was left to be brought up in the mountains by nymphs. Aphrodite returned the boy to his father when he was five and Anchises boasted about being the lover of Aphrodite. Zeus, in a fury, lamed the king with a thunderbolt for breaking his solemn word. By the time of the fall of Troy, Anchises was an old man.

In his home near Priam's palace, Aeneas slept. Creusa, his much-loved wife, lay beside him, wide awake. Suddenly Aeneas awoke and cried out. Creusa, alarmed, asked her husband what was wrong. He told her that he had seen Hector in a dream, bleeding, filthy and with a hundred open wounds. Aeneas went on to tell Creusa that Hector had told him he must leave the city and take with him the domestic gods, Creusa, his father and their dear son.

Hector went on to tell Aeneas that he would wander in the wilderness and across the sea, and that he would then found a mighty city. Aeneas was confused by the vividness of the dream. He asked Creusa what she thought it might mean.

"It means what it says, my husband. Listen to your dreams. Be ready. Just be ready."

And with that Creusa slipped from the bed and quietly began to make ready for a journey. Aeneas smiled at her and got up. Creusa was Trojan-born and wise. He washed his face and hands, kissed his wife and took up his sword and shield from near the door. He waited in the dark while outside the silent city slept. There was only the single scream of a hunting owl, then silence again.

The Trojan men slept off the effects of the celebrations, held because Troy was free at last. The Wooden Horse stood in the main square where it had been left after being dragged through the city walls. The Trojans had filled the gap with rubble and spent the rest of the night celebrating. Sinon, the Greek, walked quickly into the dark shadow under the belly of the horse. He reached up and undid the hidden wooden bolts that held the door into the hollow belly of the horse, where thirty Greek warriors, led by Odysseus had hidden. Quickly, they uncoiled a rope and slipped down into the dark Trojan street. Across the bay the Greek fleet returned from its hiding place over the horizon. Softly it inched into the shore. The Greek warriors waded to land and raced up the beach.

Some who had slipped from the belly of the horse slaughtered the guards on the walls while others opened the gates of Troy. Their comrades from the long ships slipped into the streets and spread like a plague through the sleeping city. The final battle for Troy began. It was a bloody dance of death.

ABOVE *Aeneas carries his father Anchises while Creusa his wife and his small son follow through the burning city.*

OPPOSITE *The Trojan Horse, as painted by Tiepolo c. 1760, is dragged into the city walls by an exulting crowd.*

VIRGIL

Born in 70BC in a village near Mantua, in northern Italy, Publius Vergilius Maro was the son of farmers. He had a good education and later went to Rome to study mathematics, public speaking and medicine. He then moved south to Naples and began to write poetry there. The poet Horace (65–8BC) was a friend of his.

BELOW *Virgil the Roman poet who wrote the* Aeneid, *an epic about Aeneas and his journey.*

Much of his poetry was concerned with the rural and the farming life he knew from his childhood. He finished the *Georgics* in 29BC and spent the rest of his life writing the *Aeneid*. He was fortunate in that he became a member of the court circle and was under the patronage of a senior member of the ruling group, Maecenas, who was powerful enough to give the young poet a house in Naples.

His poetry was very popular and when the Emperor Octavian defeated Mark Anthony, he suggested to Virgil that he write a celebration of the glory of Rome. Thus he began the *Aeneid*. Using *The Iliad* and *The Odyssey* as models, this epic poem takes as its subject Aeneas's journey from the devastation of Troy to his part in the founding of Rome.

Virgil travelled to Greece and met the Emperor Augustus, who was one of his patrons, in Athens. He began the journey back to Rome with him but fell ill in Megara. He struggled to get to Italy and arrived in Brindisi where he died in was 19BC aged 51.

Virgil had asked his executor to destroy the manuscript of the *Aeneid* but the emperor ordered him to ignore this request.

It was only a faint noise Aeneas heard. It came from the other side of the city square near the temple. He thought it was the changing of the watch. Still sleepy and remembering the vision he had had of Hector's face, he tried to wipe away the bloody image of his face from his mind. Then he looked again across the city and knew the truth. Two houses were blooming with fire. He knew the men who owned the houses and they were good men. Then warning trumpets sounded and people began to shout. Aeneas pulled on the rest of his armour and calmed Creusa and his son.

His wife was ready to move quickly if necessary. Aeneas warned her to barricade the doors and only to open them to him. As he spoke, Panthus, a neighbour, came rushing by carrying the statues of the gods from the temple and dragging his young grandson behind him.

"It's over," he called. "Troy is betrayed by that damned horse. The city burns and that horse stands yet in the square. That liar Sinon struts in triumph beside the empty horse, no doubt. The streets to the main gates are lined with Greek soldiers with their weapons at the ready. No one is fighting them. We are betrayed."

Without thinking, Aeneas turned and raced towards the flames. He collected other warriors as he ran, including the youth Coroebus, who had come to try and win Cassandra. She had prophesied the fate of Troy long ago and no one listened to her. Now it was too late.

Aeneas turned to the men who followed him and called out to them:

"Let us die. We can run into the thick of the fight and at least preserve our honour. There is no safety for a beaten man except that he give up hope of safety."

The Trojan men ran, mad with courage, like a pride of lions racing blind into any enemy. They abandoned all thought of their wives and children and ran into the darkness towards the flickering roaring lights of the fires. And they wept for the fall of a mighty city and its empire.

At every corner, death and fear and the clash of bronze on bronze. In the confusion Greeks mistook Aeneas and the rushing Trojans for Greeks so the Trojans, with surprise on their side, destroyed them at a stroke. Another Greek called out as if they were friends and only when he saw the Trojan faces, in the sudden burst of light from a falling building, did he back off as a man does from a striking snake. He died as his comrades did under the blades in the smoke and filth of battle.

Coroebus saw his sweetheart, Cassandra, with her wrists tied, being taken to certain slavery. He cried her name and roared into the mass of men around her. Many who followed him ran into the darkness, pinned like butterflies on the enemies' levelled spears.

The Trojans began to tear down buildings and throw them on to the enemy as they milled about the streets below. Carved and painted beams and lintels, as old as the city, crushed Greek heads and arms. Cassandra was rescued. Ajax came after Aeneas and his men in a whirlwind with his Dolopian warriors and Aeneas saw the death of Coroebus as he was slaughtered on the altar of the goddess Minerva.

The Trojans fell back, crushed by the numbers in the narrow spaces of the city. The darkness hindered all of the defenders and many, even priests, died without protection from the gods. Aeneas now witnessed the crushing of Troy and the flames in which his friends died. Neither Aeneas nor his comrades flinched from the weapons of the Greeks. If they were going to die, so be it.

From a dark street Aeneas saw Greeks rushing to Priam's palace. Aeneas and his men swept along with them, hacking and cutting. The enemy had shields locked and ladders hooked on to the walls that they climbed. The desperate Trojans were still tearing down their city stone from stone, tower by tower and hurling them on to the wall of shields below.

Yet more painted beams were flung from the highest buildings into the massed enemy below. All the time came the roar of flames and the shouts of men in anger and fear and in pain. Across the open square, the palace of Priam, who had never been kind to Aeneas, was under attack. But, whatever the slight, he was king, and it was Aeneas's duty to fight for him.

In front of the ancient palace men with double-headed axes tore down the bronze-covered doors. Through them the invaders looked into the palace of Priam that had been home to kings of Troy for generations. The guards were butchered where they stood and in poured the Greeks. Women of the house wailed with fear, and held each other in their terror as the ruthless invaders hacked down those who tried to stop them. Aeneas saw the floor running with blood. Across the sacred altar Priam lay slaughtered like a sacrifice.

Priam had seen one of his sons running across the room, to the shelter of his old arms. The boy was cut down and gutted by Achilles's son, Neoptolemus. The old king had on his armour and raised a feeble sword against the killer. Before they cut him down he warned them that what they had done was a terrible crime, for to slaughter a son in front of his own father was a sin for which the gods would demand payment. He reminded Neoptolemus that his father had treated him kindly. But Achilles's son cursed the old man and Priam, who had been king of Troy and Asia, was left headless on the altar.

Aeneas saw it all and thought then of Creusa his wife and of his son and father. He turned and hurried out of the palace and past Helen who was hiding in the shrine. She was afraid of the Trojans, who hated her for what she had brought, afraid of the Greeks for what she had done to Menelaus and afraid of all sides because she had caused them ten years of hardship at the walls of Troy. Aeneas wanted to cut her throat and took her by the hair, his bronze knife raised. Then he saw his mother, the goddess, Aphrodite, who told him to leave Helen to her fate and to see to his wife Creusa. He ran across the city, which was now covered in a pall of smoke and dust, with fires blooming and glittering from every building. It began to crumble about him as he ran. Shadows reached for him, plucked at his arms and his head; he swept them aside.

His lame father was in his house and at first refused to leave. He shamed Aeneas into turning to go back to the fight. Then wise Creusa brought his son to him and asked him to take them both so that the three of them might die together. The stones of the buildings began to crack and shatter from the heat and still men died. A light shone about the little boy's head. It was a message from the gods like the dawning Sun.

Then Aeneas understood that there was nothing more for them to do in Troy. He took a lion skin and put it over his shoulders, took up his father and held his son's hand while Creusa followed. They slipped into the dark road and, hugging the rocky walls, carefully made for a gate in the fortress walls. As they left, their home was taken by the fire and everything was lost except the household gods that Aeneas had already gathered up.

Everywhere the Greeks were looting what they could. They snatched rich cloth, cups of solid gold, bowls of bronze, jewels and precious stones as well as gold and silver from rooms and temples. Soldiers were piling the riches of Troy on the ground and around them they guarded terrified groups of women who they would use and sell later. All the wealth of mighty Troy was piled in doorways. Aeneas pitied the weeping women under guard. He tugged his son's hand and he called out for his mother.

Aeneas looked round for Creusa. His wife had vanished into the chaos of fire and smoke and roaring men. Aeneas took his son and father to a place of safety outside the city walls. He left them in the care of friends then raced back into the city calling Creusa's name. Great plumes of smoke were pouring from doors and behind the smoke was fire and he could hear the moans of wounded men and the high-pitched screams of women and the shuddering cries of children dying.

And then silence, as if waiting for something more, something terrible. And there was Creusa in front of him wreathed in smoke. She told him not to grieve for her for she would be no slave to any man. Her fate was to die with Troy.

"Don't weep for me. I am Trojan-born and married you... son of Aphrodite. Love our son. Go now. Leave my city, go and found another."

And before his eyes she vanished into smoke. Desperately he called her name. And then the mighty tower of Priam began to shake as the very foundations cracked open in the heat. The tower and Troy itself toppled into the darkness. It was over.

OPPOSITE *Troy burns around the Wooden Horse as Aeneas escapes with his father. As painted by Jan Brueghel c. 1596.*

EPILOGUE

◆◆

The story of Troy Level 7a ended in flames, so it is ironic that the story of the treasure in which Schliemann had set so much store also ended in a city consumed by flames. The gold and artefacts that were handed over to Berlin Museum in 1881 remained there until the end of the Second World War. Then, the treasure was lost to the world once more, as all around it raged fire, rape, pillage and the terrible destruction of a monumental war.

THE TREASURE VANISHES

In 1945 the war against Nazi Germany was being fought fiercely across Germany itself. The British, American and Western Allies were racing across Europe, rolling up resistance and driving the German army back from the west. From the north, the huge Russian army was advancing through territory that had recently been part of Hitler's Third Reich. This vast army was carrying with it the memory of the many atrocities that the Nazis had perpetrated throughout Russia during the war. The Russian and Slav people had been regarded as "sub-human" by the Nazis, and now these so-called sub-humans were looking for vengeance. The army was led by Marshal Zhukov, who had vast experience of fighting in cities such as Stalingrad. It was an army that had experienced the bitterness of retreat and had seen what soldiers were capable of doing to civilians who got in their way. It was an angry army and one that was not going to be defeated by German resistance as it steamrollered towards Berlin. This was going to be an assault without mercy.

Meanwhile, panic erupted in Berlin. The population was trying to work out how to save themselves from the ferocious assault that they knew was imminent and how they were going to hide what they owned so that when the conflict was over the city's survivors could rebuild their lives. In some cases, they were also working out how to protect the nation's most valuable artistic objects, some of which had been stolen on Hitler's orders. Nothing changes in times of war, whether in the age of the spear or the bomb.

The director of the Berlin Museum had already decided that many of the treasures held there, including the Schliemann collection, which was already packed into three large, sealed crates, would be hidden in a bunker in Berlin Zoo.

On April 20, 1945, the Russians arrived at the outskirts of Berlin. They waited until the city was surrounded and then began an assault that turned the once glorious city into a vision of hell. Artillery shells roared in at close range. Buildings collapsed, hydrants ruptured, fires broke out all over the city and still the shells rained down. Then the Red Army began a steady advance through the rubble.

Here was an army bent on destruction that was as savage as anything the Greeks did in Troy when it fell to them. Thirty thousand women were said to have been raped by the advancing Russian army, a revenge, perhaps, for the siege of Stalingrad in 1942–3. The invading force spread out through the city, taking on the defenders, wiping them out and rolling on.

The main building of the zoo was the site of a large gun emplacement, which became a primary target for the Russian army. Slaughtering the zoo's hippopotamus and elephants, the street fighters of Zhukov's army moved on to take the defences. As Hitler and his closest colleagues killed themselves or fled the city, the authorities that remained tried to surrender. More than a quarter of a million people lay dead and nearly every single building of note was reduced to rubble. It was indeed hell on earth.

The defenders of the zoo building surrendered on May 1, and an elite force moved in. Their work was to locate and take the most important artistic finds into protective custody. Many had vanished already, but pictures by such great artists as Degas, Manet, El Greco, Delacroix, Titian, Rubens and Botticelli were taken to Russia by this unit. Huge packing cases of ancient treasures, stone friezes, altars, Greek sculptures, jewels and other treasures vanished, never to be seen again. To prevent further looting, a German curator asked a senior Russian officer for help. He revealed that there were three sealed crates that were especially important. A Russian art expert looked into them and instantly resealed all three – the German curator never again saw the golden treasures of Troy. They vanished into the chaos of the smoking city.

The packing cases became a part of a vast convoy of loot that was sent back to Russia. Everything from typewriters to the diadem, which, according to Heinrich Schliemann, had been worn by Helen of Troy, vanished. Yet again Troy's treasure was hidden. It was lost, as surely as if it had been buried under the many layers of a small hill called Hissarlik.

Now, after years of detective work, there are hints and hopes that the treasure from the three huge crates may soon be found in Russia and that the glories of Schliemann's discoveries may be revealed once more.

Heinrich Schliemann may not have been a scholar, he may not have been scientific or meticulous and the academic establishment may have mocked and disbelieved him. But Heinrich Schliemann did prove that Troy was more than a myth.

That small hill in Turkey known as Hissarlik became a haunt of bats and foxes; briar and bramble took over and slowly it became no more than a few humps of earth and stones. Wind howled across the plain from the river, bending the few trees that were there. There was the site of ancient Troy – forgotten, unknown and abandoned, except in a story. But a man heard that story and had a dream. He dreamed of Helen of the long hair, of vain Paris, of mighty Agamemnon, Odysseus the fox and Achilles and Hector who were mighty warriors. He dreamed of the gods. He dreamed of Troy – and though much of what he supposed was wrong – he found it.

INDEX

CREDITS

——— ❖❖ ———